Yikes, you can see my underpants!

A mostly true, entirely plausible story

Part One - 1st Edition

By Francis(Frank) Treate Hogg

Part One - 1st Edition

Version 1.1

Copyright Francis Treate Hogg 2011

Website: http://www.FrankHogg.com

Check the website for updated information on works in progress and other news and resources. In addition you'll find an "Extras" page to supplement each book with information and pictures not found in the books.

Email: Frank@FrankHogg.com

Picture credits

All of the pictures were taken by family members and myself and are from a family collection of photos, slides and negatives in my possession. The front cover image is of Frank Hogg at about 3-4 years old. My father likely took it, location unknown. Yes, if you look close, you can indeed see my underpants.

Cover design and interior type and layout by Frank Hogg with the help of Apple and Pages 9.0 templates.

My Family

1950
Back row L to R, John 12, Bruce 14, Bill Jr 17.
Front row L to R, Pop or Bill Sr, Tom 7, Frank (me) 5, Mom or
Frances Hogg

Yikes, you can see my underpants!

Notes:

Yikes, you can see my underpants!

What Was Going On?

I could feel movement, could hear wheels turning on a smooth surface, could feel the cool air on my skin. I opened my eyes and the ceiling of a hallway was flashing by. People were running. I was being jostled just a little. Was this a hospital? Then the pain came back and I passed out.

Acknowledgments:

My life is made up of the people who've I've encountered along the way. Like a pinball I've bounced from one to the other each one leaving a mark on me. Who do I thank without thanking everyone, who's special, who made the biggest difference? If I name one I'll offend someone else. I won't name anyone but instead I'll name them all. But not in print, in my heart and my mind. You know who you are and I thank you.

But...

I would like to thank my good friend Jo Alderman who encouraged me and was invaluable in helping me prepare this tome for your reading pleasure. I swore her to secrecy while I was writing it just in case I didn't get it done.

And...

To Grace Kelley, who years ago encouraged me to write a book and for proofreading.

And to Peach and John Hogg for both moral support and proofreading and more things than I can count.

And to Rich Hogg for proofreading and feedback.

And to my immediate and extended family.

Behind the title, "Yikes, you can see my underpants"

Several years ago I used the cover picture of me and the title of this book for a card to send to my Aunt Adelaide, the matriarch of our family. It got a huge laugh from everyone so I thought as my life has been a fun and funny ride that this title fit well.

Then as I wrote the book I came to realize that the title meant more than that. I was bearing my soul and by the time I finish this series of books everything there is to know about me will have been exposed, as if I were standing before you in my underpants. But I won't tell absolutely everything and I won't stand in front of you naked either. It turns out to be a very fitting metaphor for a book about many of the funny and poignant moments that happened in my very interesting life.

WHAT ABOUT, "A MOSTLY TRUE, ENTIRELY PLAUSIBLE STORY"

I wanted to cover my butt is the first answer. The second is that I may remember things a little differently than my siblings do, that may show me in a better light than what they remember. Plus stories of events in the past get tempered with time. The good and funny things overshadow the bad things. I remember it hurt a lot when I broke my leg but I don't remember the pain itself.

What I've written here is all (mostly) true, nothing made up (much), everything happened (more or less) the way I wrote it… (Probably.)

Introduction

My first foray into writing was in the 1980s when I ran a computer mail order business named after me. At one point at the height on that business, Lonnie Falk, the publisher of the Rainbow magazine asked me to write a monthly column. "It will be good for business." He said. Because of that he would not pay me for it. I agreed to do it and did so for about a year. The first column was torture, it took me two days to write it and I wished I hadn't committed to it. It got easier over time and my last column only took 2 hours to write.

That was the end of my writing career until the late 1990s when while living on Song Lake in Preble, NY two things occurred at almost the same time. I was president of the lake association at the time, which was largely a social position. Song Lake is small, only 110 pieces of property on it. Perhaps that is why Song Mountain Ski Resort thought it would be easy for them to use the lakes water to make snow. That turned me into an accidental activist working to stop them.

About that time Flying J wanted to build a truck stop in town and the lake people joined forces with the group fighting Flying J. That was the beginning of a multi year fight to beat them both. That is the subject for a different book. What that did was cause me to write a lot. First handouts and flyers and then a web site in 2000, one of the first websites to play an activist role. The web changed our fight and was a major force in beating both entities.

Writing for the website became a daily thing and I wrote tens of thousands of words. At first I got complaints about my poor punctuation. One time I put a group of commas and periods at the bottom of the page for people to use as needed. In time I got better and more readable.

Then in 2008 I moved to the Radford Virginia area where my mother was born. Family history, sketchy as it was, told us that grandpa Kelley, my mothers maiden name, back around 1904 was on the city council and had something to do with tree planting in the city. The house he built on Wadsworth Street and the store he ran across the street are still there. When I looked in the municipal building for more information I found very little and no proof of the trees or city council. The property information was there and that helped fill in the blanks but nothing else.

I looked at the town meeting records to see if they would show anything. They are hand written in now faded black ink on paper turning brown and extremely hard to read. I decided to go back one day and make photos of the pages so I could use a computer to make that job easier. I have to admit I was a little disappointed that I found nothing else until one day I was looking through two small piles of 100 year old documents. I found a voter sign in sheet with my grandfathers signature written in his hand. That was just a small thing but it was actual proof that he was really there and all the stories, while not proven, had the possibility of being true.

Besides that signature and a few faded pictures there is nothing to show that he ever existed. We are his only heritage, his legacy and that's typical I guess.

I don't have any kids, no one to carry on my name. Once I am gone there will be little to nothing to show I was ever here or what I was like. That's the main reason I'm writing this book. I started it back in 2005 and stopped after not much more than a brief outline. I picked it up again recently and have been working on it ever since.

Looking through boxes of old photos for this book brought back memories and made me realize even more how I wanted to leave my mark. Everyone wants that, something to be remembered by. Big shots have buildings and roads named after them. Parents name their children after them. As the last and youngest child I was named after my mother Frances. Thankfully my name is spelled Francis with the 'i' making all the difference, at least to me.

Many people leave no mark at all, nothing to show they were here. As I looked at those photos I wondered who these people were. Many had no writing on them and for all I know these photos were all the mark they left. Made me kind of sad to think that.

I've led an interesting and fun life and have many stories to pass on that I hope you will find interesting and amusing. They will likely remind you of your own childhood and what it was like. Maybe you'll even write a book to pass on to your kin. We all have family stories we tell at Thanksgiving and Christmas, whenever the family gets together. Over time they get better, embellished as it were, to be funnier or to inflict more pain on the victim. All of what you read here are things that really happened, mostly true and entirely plausible. Tested by years of story telling at family gatherings and honed to a fine edge. All of it governed by that all encompassing term, "Artistic License."

This story telling is true of most families, not just mine.

This book is just part of my life that covers what it was like growing up in 1950s Scranton, the move to Syracuse in

1958 and my teenage years there. There were two hurricanes, Hazel and Diane, broken legs and ribs and other maladies. Most of all it's about fun, life, death, the importance of family and the human condition.

This is just the beginning. In future works I plan to cover my adult life. Owning an appliance store and going bankrupt, becoming a contractor then a dental technician then owning my own lab, then owning a computer business in the heyday of the 80's. Building my own house. The fight to beat a ten billion dollar corporation and how a small but determined group of people won it and where I ended up. I think I've led an interesting and unusual life and I hope you enjoy reading about it as much as I enjoyed writing it

My Mission in Life

I asked my Mom why there was an 8 year gap between my brother Tom and John. The three oldest brothers were Bill Jr, Bruce and John.

Mom told me quite frankly that, "Dad's hunting trip to Canada to bag that moose upset me and to make things right he bought me a fur coat and that resulted in Tom."

"Okay" I said, "That explains that, Tom was a mistake, why did you have me two years later?"

"I wanted you to keep Tom company," she said.

"So my reason for existence was to keep a mistake company?" I asked.

"Yes," she said smiling…

This is the infamous fur coat that was the appeasement for my fathers moose hunting trip to Canada. I don't know who to thank for my existence, the moose, the fur coat or Tom.

The Sneak-A-Peek

We lived on Taylor Ave until I was five years old. Being that young I don't remember much but I do remember we had a maid, a very pretty girl or so I thought at the time. She was probably a teenager at best and her parents lived out in the country. Years later while driving in that area my parents stopped and we visited with her. She had turned into a beautiful woman.

Back when she was taking care of us a plot was brewing.

I have 4 older brothers. Tom +2 years, John +8 years Bruce +12 and Bill +16. When I was 5 John was 12 and Bruce was 17 and very interested in the maid. We have no sisters so the maid was the only female in the house besides my Mom. Our house had a second floor balcony that went all the way across the back and one of the windows was into the bathroom. Many times my brothers tried and failed to sneak a peek at the maid while she bathed. So, they went for the next best thing.

The took me aside and 'suggested' I should barge in on her while she was bathing and then tell them what I saw. I was to get a good look so I could report everything. Hell, I was five, what did I know. They waited until the maid had gone in and after an appropriate amount of time they sent me in. I opened the door and went in. The maid was already in the tub and I couldn't see a damn thing. I was five remember and not tall enough to see much over the rim of the tub or if I saw anything I wouldn't know what it was. She threw her wash cloth at me and told me to get out. The Two Musketeers then grilled me for every detail.

"What did you see when she threw the wash cloth at you?" They said.

"Nothing, I ducked" I said.

"Before that, could you see her nip-, I mean her chest?" They said.

"No, she was under the water." I said.

"Well, hell, did you at least see a bare knee?" They said.

"No," I said.

"Don't tell Mom about this or you'll get in trouble." They said.

"Okay," I said.

The next day while my brothers were outside playing the maid took me aside and asked me if my brothers put me up to coming in while she was taking a bath. I said yes, after all they didn't say I couldn't tell the maid. She smiled and said she could hear them outside the bathroom window trying to look in and when she didn't hear them she thought they were up to something. She seemed tickled they would do that. Me, I was five and didn't have a clue why all this was going on.

~~~

For some reason my Dad decided to replace the railing on the rear balcony. It was probably rotted. The neighborhood girls took the balusters and like you would with match sticks, they built a box around my brother John. He's a calm type and didn't seem to mind but when they got to the height of his head and wanted to cover it up he decided to break it all down. They giggled and acted stupid as they usually did. There were always girls around my brothers, good looking bunch that they were. Me too I guess. I made a cute looking kid. Even made the cover of a book. :)

The Sports Car with No Floor

One day a friend of my Dad's came over to show him his new sports car. It looked more like a racer than anything. I never saw anything like it. Tear dropped body with the wheels outside of it and no fenders. They took me for a ride which scared the hell out of me because there was no floor. All I could do was stare terrified at the pavement rushing by below me and try to keep from falling while my Dad kept telling me to calm down. I guess I must have been frantic and probably crying too. Looking back on it I think my Dad was watching me while Mom was out because she would not have let him go for a ride much less take me in such a dangerous car. So, I guess he had to take me if he wanted to ride in it. Pop was smart because he didn't tell me not to tell Mom which would have made me tell her. I was the youngest of five boys and he had much experience keeping things from Mom.

ROOT BEER IN THE BASEMENT, TOASTER LIKE A CONVEYOR BELT, AND MY DAD THE PHOTOGRAPHER

Even though kids five and under aren't supposed to remember their childhood I have many memories of living on Taylor Avenue. I remember my grandmother teaching me how to make a peanut butter sandwich.

"Spread the peanut butter all the way to the edge and the same for the jelly too. Put the jelly on the other slice of bread, not on top of the peanut butter" she told me.

To this day I do it that way, be it ingrained habit or programming. I don't even like it when someone makes me a PB&J and doesn't do it that way.

We had an unusual toaster. It was long and thin with a conveyor belt that you put the bread on. My job in the morning was to feed the toaster. The bread came out the other end perfectly done because there were no hot spots. I recently saw one like it on an antique show about a guy who collected toasters. It was quite a pleasure seeing it again.

My Dad made homemade root beer in the basement. We had a complete setup including a machine with a long black handle to press the bottle cap on the bottle. There was a box of new bottle caps and you would place the bottle in the holder, put the cap lightly on in and pull the handle down to crimp it. It looked easy and I wanted to do it but I was too small to work the handle. But the root beer was good.

Singing for my Dinner

At 5 I had a very high voice and my Mom entered me into the boys choir. We would go down to the hall where we practiced and sing in a room off to the side. That room was always dingy, with cheap metal chairs and not very well lit and not very warm.

Bless This House

Bless this house, O Lord we pray,
Make it safe by night and day . . .

Bless these walls so firm and stout,
Keeping want and trouble out . . .

Bless the roof and chimneys tall,
Let thy peace lie overall . . .

Bless this door that it may prove,
Ever open,
To joy and love . . .

Bless these windows shining bright,
Letting in God's Heavenly light,
Bless the hearth, the painting there,
With smoke ascending like a prayer!

Bless the folk who dwell within,
Keep them pure and free from sin . . .

Bless us all that we may be,
Fit O Lord to dwell with thee . . .

Bless us all that one day we may dwell,
O Lord! With Thee!

My mother would sit and watch me with the pride of a mother. I was the youngest of 5 boys and named after her, the baby of the family. The three oldest were teenagers and as teenagers are what they are, she preferred the sweet innocence of a child like me. Besides the choir she took me to charm school where I learned how to ask a girl to dance the foxtrot and good manners. I was too young and it didn't take. The boys and girls would sit along the wall of the dance floor, girls to the left, boys to the right. Then the teacher would tell the boys to ask a girl to dance. All the boys would head to this one pretty blond girl and I followed along because I didn't know what else to do. I never got to dance with her and usually ended up with the girl nobody else wanted. She was fat and much taller than me. I was still small so I never got the pretty ones.

In later years I got saddled with piano lessons that was also a waste of time. I would walk down this long alley near our house to the woman who taught piano. She had me sit there doing these incredibly boring exercises that did not inspire me to play. Then I'd give her the money my mother gave me for the lesson and escaped. I don't remember a thing from that. Musically I just wasn't into it. My day in the arts came and went with the choir.

We were practicing, "Bless This House" because we were going to sing it on TV, which in the 50's was just getting started and was very crude. The first thing I ever saw on the TV my Dad brought home was, "Cookla, Fran and Ollie" a puppet show. The quality was so bad you had to use your imagination to think you saw what was there. It was novel and new and so much better than radio.

We arrived at the TV studio to sing on a show that featured a clown character who would get kids up on his lap and talk to them. When I watched it on TV it seemed like he was in a big room. We walked into the studio and it was small.

Have you ever gone back to places you were at when you were a kid and while they seemed big as a child they now seemed small. Well, I was already small and this studio seemed small to me. About the size of a small bedroom and the door took up a major part of the wall. As we came in there was a display of bakery snacks, maybe Tasty Cake or something like that. Buns covered with sticky frosting and other things I salivated over when I saw them on TV. In the studio because of the hot bright lights they looked like they were made of wood. I put my finger out and touched one and sure enough, wood. They didn't look very tasty in person but TV in those days was so bad you couldn't tell.

We were ushered to the far wall where they had boards for us to stand on. Being small I got the front row with two more rows behind me. We stood about 5 kids wide and took up half the back wall.

All the while we were doing that and being hushed by a TV person the clown was putting these kids, some littler than me on his lap and asking silly questions, "How are you little girl?" and crap like that.

I looked up at the ceiling and saw banks of lights, all turned off. There must have been 20 of them in big aluminum reflectors that covered the ceiling. Then it came our time to sing. The clown introduced us and the single large camera, in the small room, swung around and the lights came on. It was like walking out of a dark basement into bright sunlight and heat lamp hot. I closed my eyes and turned my head down in reaction and all of us got off to a shaky start because of it.

Bless this house, O Lord we pray

We croaked it out and finished more or less together. At one point I could see the camera's large black eye looking right at me and I didn't like it at all.

When we finished they killed our lights and put more lights on the pastry display, the camera swung around to look down at that really close up and we were ushered out of the room with the TV guy holding his finger to his lips to hush us up.

I didn't watch that show much after that. The mystery was gone and the appeal too.

That my friends, ended both my TV and singing career. I never looked back either.

Thankfully YouTube wasn't around then.

Pops Business

(May 1, 1947)

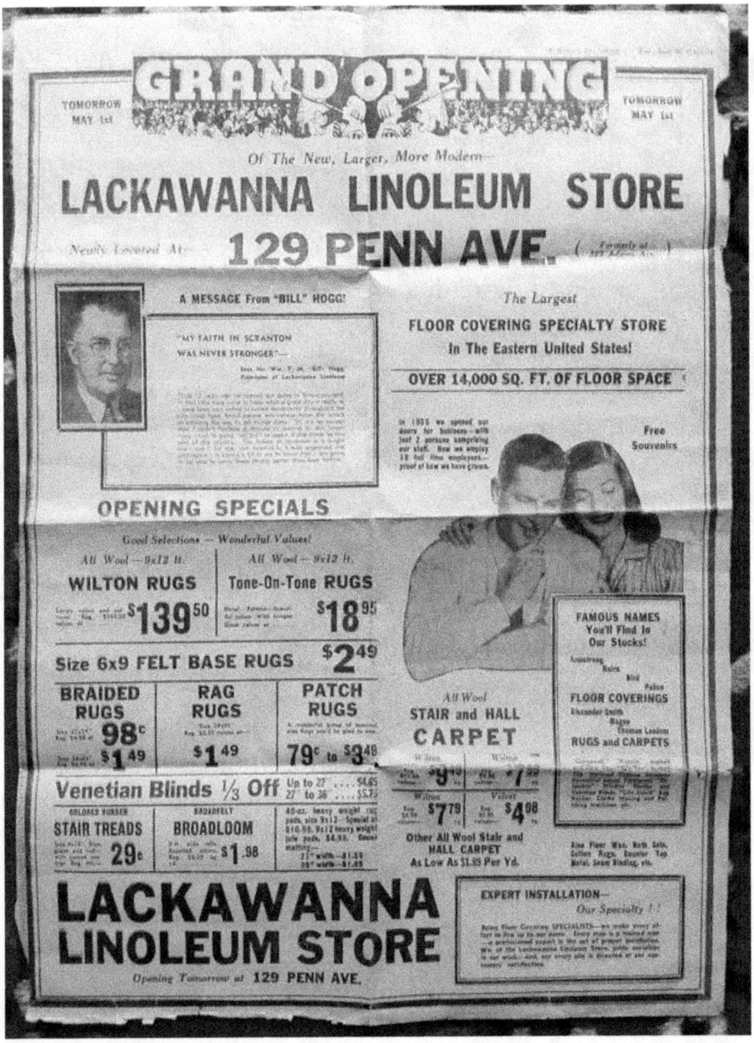

Bankrupt!

In 1950 my Dad's 18 year old business, Lackawanna Linoleum Store did a big job for an apartment complex. They put plastic tile, fashionable at the time, in all the bathrooms. The cement made by Armstrong failed and Armstrong would only cover the cost of replacing the cement. Replacing all the tile put my Dad into bankruptcy. I remember a box of cement encrusted tile in the basement and my Dad asking me if I could scrap the cement off them so he could use them again. I was too young to do it very well but I sure tried. I wonder why he didn't sue Armstrong. In later years when I asked him about it he didn't want to talk about it. After that he got a job working for a carpet company near Scranton selling on the road. He became a manufacturers rep and did that job until the day he died.

Going broke meant we had to move out of the Taylor Street house into 1716 Linden Street and after that to 314 Irving Ave. The Linden Street house is still there as are all the houses we lived in in Scranton. Truth is, we bounced around a lot. Main Street was another place we lived. The problem with all this moving is I kept going to different schools and didn't have the group of friends that many people have who attended one school until they graduated. I visited the Linden Street house a few years ago and it's now a credit union. I was glad to see they didn't destroy the beautiful oak entrance with the stairway going to the second floor. The dining room, where we put the Christmas tree when we didn't put it in the front hall, was now a conference room. The house on Irving Ave is still there but the neighborhood has run down since we lived there. The

Main Street house seems to be there but when I visited I couldn't tell exactly which one it was.

I remember one day when I was seven or so a man came to our back door selling the largest apples I had ever seen. He showed my mother one of the apples and then took it in his large hands and twisted it cleanly top to bottom in two even pieces. He gave my mother one to taste and she bought a bushel of them. To this day I have never seen anyone split an apple like that.

Nay Aug Park

Nay Aug Park is the largest park in Scranton, Pennsylvania, It had a amusement park that closed in the 1990s. The park has a small zoo, the Nay Aug Gorge, the Everhart Museum, and two Olympic-sized swimming pools. Back when I was a kid it was one big pool. More information can be found at:

http://www.nayaugpark.org/

MY FIRST BIKE

My first bicycle was a 20" job and I had trouble keeping up with the other kids who had bigger wheels on their bikes. Before I could get a bike I had to show my father I could ride one. Training wheels were unheard of in my circle. Every time I tried to borrow one of the other kids' bikes I would have trouble, crash it and after a while no one would lend me their bike to try. Determined and desperate

I knew a kid who just got a new bike and I knew he wasn't home.

I went over to his house and asked his mother if I could take the bike, I lied and said her son said it was okay. To my surprise and relief she said yes and I was all set. I walked the bike until I was out of sight of their house and then I mounted the beast determined to learn how to ride.

The alley where he lived was reasonably flat but it sloped downhill to a cross street at the bottom. My plan was to use the hill to avoid having to peddle which should make it easier to learn how to ride. I started off a little shaky but I was determined and while I almost hit a car on one side and the wall on the other, I managed to get in under control. After a few hundred feet I was feeling pretty good. I even tried peddling a bit but by then the hill was getting steep and I was going faster and faster. At that point I realized for the first time that I didn't know how to brake. The bottom of the hill was fast approaching and I was getting desperate so I decided to bail out and worry about the damage to the bike later. As I stood up on the peddle I found the brakes and came to a skidding halt very close to the moving cars.

A guy yelled at me for being reckless as I rode shakily off. I rode around awhile to get the hang of it and then rode home to show my Dad I knew how to ride, and that's how I got my little bike.

Now I could play with the other kids, now I was part of the gang. At about the same time I got my bike they paved Linden Street where I lived and while the road was blocked off to car traffic we were able to ride our bikes freely on the street.

I stopped by a telephone pole to rest and this old man, who looked like a bum, was walking down the sidewalk. He paused by the pole, put one finger to his right nostril, sucked in and out in several short quick breaths and then blew out quickly and let fly a perfectly rounded green snot from his left nostril, that landed at the base of the pole. A very impressive trick that probably grossed you out but this is the kind of stuff that little boys thrive on. Impressed with the prowess of the snot blowing old man I practiced for long hours but I was never able to master the trick. It's a pity too because I'm old now and I'm sure I could impress many young boys if only I had become a, "Snot Blowing Master".

The gang and I tired of the new road and took a short ride over to Nay Aug park. The park had many winding paths through grassy areas and fancy flower beds. One of the paths led down a slight hill to the duck pond which was surrounded by a very low stone curb, perhaps 4 inches high. I raced behind the other kids going as fast as I could, trying my best to keep up.

The duck pond was a round affair with a fountain in the middle, surrounded by a low stone wall perhaps 4 inches high. It was made of flagstone like so many things in Scranton. At one spot the wall was very short and one stone was at an angle almost like a jump and only a couple inches high. We got the harebrained idea of riding down the path and jumping the stone ramp out into the pond. We dared and taunted each other and I took the bait, ah... I mean challenge. I peddled up the path to make my run. I wanted to see how far out into the pond I could go so I peddled real fast and hit the stone jump at great speed.

It was like in slow motion as I slowly rotated in the air and landed upside down in the pond holding onto the bike with a death grip. The pond was only waist deep and about 6 inches of muck, or duck crap, on the bottom. I waded back to the edge and my buddies helped me lift the bike out after they were through laughing. I sat on the edge of the wall taking my shoes and socks off to rinse out the gunk. The bike survived the incident without harm and I soon dried off while my friends threw rocks at the ducks.

We rode over to the big artificial lake where everybody could swim. The lake had concrete beaches around three-fourths of the way and was very shallow on one end and very deep on the other. I was walking around the deep end wall and as I walked past the lifeguard tower, I saw this little kid, only a foot from the edge flaying in the water because he couldn't swim. Back then they didn't paint the pool walls and bottom blue so the water was black, foreboding and deep. The lifeguard didn't see the kid because he was looking at the big kids jumping and diving off the diving board some distance away. So I reached down, grabbed the kids arm and pulled him out. He coughed a bit and ran off. Did I save a life or just help a kid out? Guess I'll never know.

In the winter when the lake froze over, people would come out and skate. There was always a group of 4 to 8 speed skaters who would skate around the perimeter in single file, their left hand behind their backs as they stroked in fascinating unison. Left foot, right foot, their right arm swinging, they were as one and it was fascinating to watch. I made several attempts to learn how to skate but the ice was hard and cold and my butt was soft and warm, so I never went very far with it.

I joined up with my friends and we rode on over to the arcade.

At the time I thought the arcade was really cool but looking back on it now it was ... well ... tacky. I really liked the pinball machines but they didn't have any new ones like the drugstore downtown. Theirs were the old two penny ones and they were really worn. Sometimes you could get a free play if you jiggled it just right. Two pennies was in my price range too. It was either play the pinball machine or buy those red silver dollars to eat on the way home. More often than not I would choose the pinball machine. They also had other old machines. I liked the one that gave you a postcard with a random picture of an air force jet on it. At the front of the arcade you could get cotton candy, soda and stuff or buy a ticket to ride on the carousel or the small kids train. That stuff was too childish for us big kids with bikes and we wandered off to find new challenges.

We rode over to the woods behind Nay Aug park and left our bikes by a trail that led down into the woods. We walked down to the cliffs above the railroad tracks and talked about rigging a rope from one side of the gorge to the other as if we really could do something like that. One boy said his father had all the stuff we would need and we argued and planned for hours about how we were going to do this. We discussed the possibility of building a rocket that would pull the rope across the gorge and considered a section of wire first as the flame from the rocket would burn the rope. Much discussion went into aiming and we decided that someone would have to be on the other side to catch the rope so it wouldn't fall back into the gorge. No one wanted the job of rocket catcher so we just sat there and couldn't come up with any other ideas.

Then we wandered back up the path to a dead stump and sat on the nearby rocks when one of us commented how similar the stump was to a fireplace. It was rotted and hollow and had a hole near the bottom at one spot. We got some twigs and leaves and started a fire in the rotted stump. It didn't take long before the fire was roaring and we tried but couldn't put it out so we ran back up the path and grabbed our bikes and high tailed it out of there. By the time we got back to the park the fire engine sirens could be heard and we could see a lot of smoke coming from the woods. Lucky for us they put it out quickly and we never got caught. For some reason we forgot all about stringing the rope across the gorge. Thank God for that.

25 Cent Movie Every Saturday

Every Saturday we would go to the theater on Main Street. My Mom would give us each a quarter which would get us into the movie and sometimes a dime or two for a snack. I never wanted to spend the snack money at the theater but would save it and stop at the Dolly Madison dairy which was also on Main Street and on my way home. The ice cream seemed much better back then than it does now, maybe it's just because it was such a rare treat and not a staple as it seems today.

The movie's feature film was usually a cowboy film, Roy Rogers or someone like that. What we really came for were the serials. These were short films that resolved the cliff hanger from last week and ended with another cliff hanger to be resolved next week. It never occurred to us then that we were being manipulated by "the man" who suckered us into coming back week after week. Along with those there was, "MovieTone News" which was breaking news for the week. TV news back then was limited, so much of the news came in the paper, radio or, "MovieTone News" at the theater. There was also a cartoon to round out the day.

On our way to the movie we would speculate and pose theories about last weeks cliffhanger and how it would be resolved. On the way home we would marvel about how it was resolved and wonder how our hero would get himself out of the perilous predicament he's gotten into.

If we didn't have any money we would just look in the window at Dolly Madison and salivate. If we had money, then inside we'd go and spend quite some time deciding what to get.

Swimming at the Indoor Pool Center

Our Main Street house was on the other side of town from Nay Aug park so to go swimming we would walk through vacant lots and woods to get to the center. This was an indoor swimming pool, the only one in Scranton. We paid a dime to swim for an hour or two. Mom usually gave me the dime and an extra 2 cents for some candy on the way home. The center wasn't much different from a standard Olympic sized pool but without the frills you see today. I loved to swim and could give a fish a run for it's money back then. Today I have to be careful not to be fish food.

Making the long walk home after the swim, with our wet bathing trunks rolled up in our wet towels was softened by the 2 cents for the candy store.

The candy store was a small dark shop run by an old man and not far from the center. Everything was dark about it, from the dark green paint on the outside to the dark interior. The only thing in the shop was the glass front candy case. He had very few customers and was often in the back when we came in. I guess he lived in the back of the shop, a very common practice back then. I would pick out 2 Dollar Candy at a penny each. Dollar was a gummy candy much like Juicy Fruits or Dots but they were red, a mysterious flavor that might have been cherry but the exact flavor was kind of hard to determine. It was in the shape of a dollar coin and about ⅛ inch thick. I would bite little pieces and hold them in my mouth until they melted and if I was very careful they would last me all the way home.

BROKEN PEANUT STICKS FOR A DIME

We would go to the YMCA every week for a swim, maybe play ping pong in the activity room afterwards. The changing room or locker was a little strange. Not by the room itself, but by the inhabitants. Men could come in off the street and get a shower there, some very odd men. One old man had elephantitis balls which are just huge nuts. Grapefruit sized. I watched in fascination as he showered and then dried himself off. He must have been used to it as he ignored me. I didn't know at the time it was called, "Elephantitis balls" or what caused it. It was just one of those visions that never leaves you.

We always stopped at the bakery on the way home. The smell got you when you walked out of the YMCA's door, such a delicious smell of a bakery. You could buy a bag of broken peanut sticks for a dime which was a lot cheaper that the price of just one whole one.

I would go in and press my nose against the showcase and salivate over the delicious looking eclairs and fancy cupcakes but I only had a dime and I needed to make the most of it. It was always crowded and the woman behind the counter always knew what I wanted and would go in the back room to get them for me.

I wondered why they had so many broken ones and one day I sat outside with my treasure and noticed I could put some of them back together. I think she was going into the back room and breaking them to give them to me for a dime. It pays to be a cute kid.

Thank you peanut stick woman, I'll never forget the kindness you showed and I hope you didn't get in trouble for it.

Elizabeth and Me, Sitting in a Tree

You show me yours and I'll show you mine she said. We climbed into a tree in the vacant lot on the corner so we couldn't be seen. I was unsure of doing this and very embarrassed but after she coaxed me I relented and showed her mine. She then showed me hers. I felt cheated as she didn't have much to show compared to me.

"What do you do with that?" I asked.

"I pee with it, same as you." She said.

"How do you aim it?" I asked.

She just got mad and climbed down from the tree and left. Some time later I got it into my mind that that thing of hers was lined with sandpaper and I sure didn't want to put my thing in that. I don't know where I got that idea, my brothers perhaps, I was young then, perhaps 7 or so. It kept me a virgin much longer than it should have. I found out it isn't lined with sandpaper and I spent the good or maybe even the better part of my life trying to put my thing in there as often as possible. As my years advance and my testosterone levels decline the desire has abated slightly but the memory, the oh so sweet sweet memory of doing it lingers on.

What the Fluck?

I first heard the word in the schoolyard, or should I say misheard it. I had no idea what it meant but it sounded like a good way to tell someone off. "Go fluck yourself" was what I thought I heard and I would go around telling people that. That wasn't all. I also learned to, "Give the finger" which done properly is holding up just the middle finger. I misunderstood that too and would make a fist and from that extend my middle finger. As a special touch I made an innovation, an update so to speak where I would move my middle finger to the first knuckle the adjacent fingers making what I called "the balls." I was very proud of my balls and if anyone didn't like it I would just tell them to, "Go fluck yourself!"

Now under normal circumstances that wouldn't be a big deal but when you combine 'fluck' with it, it opened me up for ridicule.

"He can't even say it right and look at the way he gives you the finger, That isn't the right way to do it, ha ha ha." was what they said.

It was some time before I learned to leave the "L" out. So to all those who made fun of me in the schoolyard. Imagine I'm extending my middle finger to you right now and you can, "Go fuck yourselves!"

Monkey Shines

One day my brother Tom, my next door neighbor Bobbie, and I were playing in the back yard. It was a small yard enclosed by a wire fence down the left side and a clump of trees on the right. Near the back porch was a flagstone patio. Flagstone was prevalent in Scranton back then. They even made sidewalks with it. I used to enjoy walking on them and seeing how every stone was a little different from the one before. If you looked close you could see things in the grain of the stone, a face, an animal, perhaps a map to buried treasure. One of my friend's father welded a dime to a spike and 'nailed' it into a crack in one of the sidewalk stones. We enjoyed laughing at people trying to pick up that dime. Near the porch, over the flagstone patio was an upside down U shaped clothes line holder, made out of pipe. Just the one near the house remained, the other end gone. We used to jump up and swing like monkeys from the pipe that made up the cross piece.

One day my brother Tom got the idea to put a chair near the pipe and jump to the pipe from the chair. This was great fun and we moved the chair farther and farther away to test ourselves. It was my misfortune to be the first to miss and do a belly flop on the flagstone patio with my face leading the way. I sat up and brushed the small leaves from my face. I didn't cry until I realized that the 'leaves' was really blood. I remember wondering at the time why I was crying because it was blood. It didn't hurt and I wasn't crying when I thought it was leaves but I cried anyway until my mother came and took me inside scolding Tom for putting me up to it. I guess I cried because I was 'supposed' to cry. I never did figure that out.

The Big Culm Dump Slide

Across the street from my house at 843 N. Main Street is a path to Powderly Court which runs above the railroad tracks down below. At one point someone had dumped dirt down the embankment that we played in. We dug tunnels, made forts that kind of thing. That day there was a pile of empty cardboard boxes stacked there and we started playing with them. We discovered that we could make a toboggan with them by opening up the box and laying it down and bringing up the front by our feet. We used these and slid down the embankment as if it were snow.

After a while we tired of the small embankment and went looking for greater challenges. That's when someone, probably me, thought that sliding down the culm dumps would be a great idea.

Culm is the waste coal from coal mining. It's still coal but only has about 60% the energy of coal, but it can burn. It's discarded in huge piles called the culm dumps. Some of the culm dumps were on fire, a fire that started before I was born and continued to smolder for years afterwards. Obviously we weren't fool enough to slide down one of those in a flammable cardboard box. Besides there wasn't a burning one nearby. We picked a new one near a coal mine not far away.

The new one had the advantage of the culm being new and jagged and the bottom was at a sharp angle to the ground rather than a smooth transition that would make it at least possible to do what I was about to do. However, this would have required foresight that I didn't have. We did consider the jagged rocks and doubled the thickness of the cardboard. It was not enough.

The steepness of the culm dump was the exact angle the pyramids are made. It turns out that if you pile sand up it will naturally pile to the same angle as the pyramids. Culm does the same thing. Just as the pyramids do the culm ends abruptly when it gets to the ground, the very hard ground, not to say the culm was soft in comparison, merely that the culm was loose.

Oblivious to this and other dangers to my body I climbed aboard the doubled cardboard sled, pulled the front up over my feet and started down the hill. It was very rough and it immediately became apparent that two thicknesses of cardboard were not near enough. I kept moving around on the cardboard as each spot I sat on wore through. My speed picked up due to the steepness of the hill and the cardboard wore out faster and faster. That was the least of my worries as I realized in horror that the ground wasn't going to be gentle and I couldn't do a thing about it.

The next thing I knew was my buddies standing over me looking down. The collision with mother earth had knocked me out. One of my buddies was holding the tattered remains of my 'sled' and the other was just laughing.

"Boy, you were really moving." He said

"What did it feel like?" The other asked.

They were obviously impressed with my feat and I couldn't let this bragging opportunity pass, so I bragged about it. We walked back home carrying the battered remains of my sled and I retold them of the ride repeatedly each time finding some new twist to brag about. It was tough to walk for a while because my butt hurt more than anything else. We kept the cardboard sled around the house for a while but someone threw it in the trash. My trophy was gone, my bragging diminished until now.

My parents never knew about it but if they had my Dad would have used one of his classic lines, "That was a damn fool thing to do!"

I can't count the number of times I heard him say that to me. He was right, it was a damned fool thing to do.

OLD BRIDGE ACROSS ROARING BROOK, PIPE BOMB AND ROCKETS

The bridge, now long gone, was once a one lane bridge across Roaring Brook high above Nay Aug Gorge. They put big iron pipes at the entrances to block cars but it was okay for walking and biking. It was a rusty trestle bridge painted grey where there was paint and rust where there wasn't. We used it to get to the other side up where kids could do things far away from supervision. We set off fireworks and built fires and all kinds of things. One day a kid I barely knew would set off a pipe bomb there.

He wasn't trying to blow something up other than the bomb and nobody knew anything about pipe bombs back then. He just took a length of pipe, filled it with gun powder and capped both ends. We heard that he built a small fire and put the bomb in it and waited for it to go off. He was too close when it did explode, and we read about him in the papers the next day. Naturally my mother thought that because I knew him I would do the same thing.

Not exactly, but close.

My brother Tom came up with this gem. We took two orange juice cans and soldered the open ends together. Cans back then were made of metal. Then we took a piece of a can and made a nose cone and soldered it to the top. We even put some fins on the side so it really looked a bit like a rocket.

Next we stole some shotgun shells from my Dad's gun cabinet and took them apart to get the gunpowder out of them. We then made a small hole in the bottom and carefully put all the gunpowder in it. We didn't have a fuse and our repeated attempts to light it failed.

Then we remembered what the pipe bomb kid did and we built a fire under it. However, we got far away and behind a large rock before it went off. Our rocket did go up in the air, or at least parts of it anyway, so you could call it a success of sorts, and we're both still here, intact to tell about it.

MY MEMORIES OF THE NAY AUG ARCADE

The arcade was old when I was a kid. There were rows of old 2 penny pinball machines lining the main hall on the side next to the bumper car area. Some of them were so old that a properly placed whack could get you a free game. The manager always kept an eye on us to make sure we paid. I played a lot of pinball but those old machines had groves and bumpers that often didn't work and it took a dedicated player to put up with it.

They also had other machines to take your money. One would take your penny and flatten it to a football shape with the Statue of Liberty impressed on it. I liked the one where you squeezed the handles to see how strong you were and the one with cards of US Air Force planes printed on them.

Next to the arcade building was a small train track for little kids, smaller than me, that rode around in a big oval. Inside the oval was a paddock where you could get a ride on a pony. I did try that once. Not very exciting as the handler was there guiding the pony with no chance to gallop away like The Lone Ranger.

All that's gone now as well as the poop flinging monkeys at the zoo and the zoo too. Tilly the elephant was a must see everytime we visited and it was a sad day for Scranton when she had to be put down due to an aggressive foot infection in 1966. Although the records are contradictory on that. Some say she was put down because she supposedly attacked her keeper. By 1966 I was living in Syracuse and only heard about it from relatives.

BUMS, HOBO CAMPS

When you hang around trains and train tracks you will occasionally run across hobos or bums. Men who hop trains and live in little encampments they made in the woods by the tracks. We ran into one of these camps but nobody was there. The little structures we found were made from found and discarded items. An old car hood made a roof on one with car seats inside for a bed. Things like that. Being stupid kids we trashed the place. Today those bums would be called homeless people, victims of society's strict rules of conduct. They were bums back then and to be avoided.

FLASHERS IN THE WOODS

One time as I was walking in the park, a man flashed me. It was just like in a cartoon, he opened his coat to show me his stuff. We laughed at him and taunted him and he ran away. He was kinda foolish doing that especially seeing he had nothing much to brag about. Another time in the woods a bum with an erection showed it to us and tried to get us to come closer. Him we ran away from. There was little fear he could catch us. Have you ever tried to run with a hard on?

JUMPING TROLLEY CARS

We jumped many trains, enough so it became common place and a natural way to travel. Scranton had trolleys back then that ran by electricity provided by overhead wires. The rack on top of the trolley car is called a catenary. The trolleys themselves were designed to make them hard to hold onto but we tried. The problem was two fold. Because it was just the one car it was hard not to be seen by the conductor so the only way you could do it was to wait till it started moving and then try to jump on the rear bumper and hold onto something all the while staying low enough not to be seen through the back window. If you managed to pull that off then is was difficult to hold on or hang on. The main reason we didn't do it much was because the trolley wasn't going anywhere we wanted to go. When all is said and done it was just easier to walk.

HOPPING AUTOMOBILE BUMPERS IN THE WINTER

This is something that would be difficult to do today for several reasons. Perhaps it would be better to explain why it worked back in my youth. First Scranton didn't use salt on the roads so they ended up being hard packed snow. As a coal mining town cinders were plentiful and they used that on hills, not on flat streets. Second, cars had bumpers which you could grab onto. The idea was to pick a street where the snow was nicely packed and wait around the corner from a stop sign. A likely victim car would stop and then slowly start off on the packed snow. As it went by we would run out and grab the rear bumper, squat down and let it pull us sliding along. It worked better with women drivers because they were less likely to expect it. Men drivers probably did it when they were kids. They would often stop and yell or worse yet speed up leaving us sprawling all over the road. We didn't do it to get anywhere, we did it because it was fun.

Stoking Coal

Scranton was and still is to some degree a coal mining town. Growing up my brothers and I took turns hauling the ash cans out to the street every week. We had to go to the basement before going to bed and upon waking up to stoke the furnace and load in more coal. The coal was delivered through a door in the riser of the front steps, down a chute to the coal bin. Usually we got a ton or two at a time. The people who could afford them had augers that ran in a pipe and automatically drew coal into the fire at an assigned rate. The systems both worked fine as long as the coal got to the furnace. If one of us screwed up the house got cold and it took a long time to warm up.

We moved into a new house on Main Street which had the access to the coal bin in the back yard. Our first load of coal was delivered when the ground was soft making roadways and tunnels for me to play in.

I really got into building those tunnels and when I ran out of them I moved up to the big time… Roads.

Our front yard had a big tree and the grass was very sparse. I used the areas of ground as a series of roads in my little city. Then I decided to "pave" them and dug up some dirt, sifted it through a piece of screen, mixed with water and paved my roads with this mud. After it dried I had the most wonderful city with it's paved streets and little neighborhoods. I had a great time playing there the rest of that day and looked forward to playing with it the next day. I went to bed dreaming of improvements I would make and drifted off to sleep.

That night it rained. All my roads were washed away but by the time the ground dried out I was on to other interests. I can add, "Road Builder" to my kid resume.

THE DAY SCRANTON GOT NATURAL GAS

After decades Scranton decided to turn off the coal and switch to gas. It's cleaner and easier to deal with. Scranton spent quite some time installing underground pipes all over town. Then they installed tall pipes at every intersection to act as purging vents while they cleared all the air out of the lines. The day came for the big turn on and they had someone at each pipe to light the gas. It was going to be a big deal so we got up very early in the morning to check it out. We walked around the neighborhood and saw all the preparations. There were trucks and men at each intersection and they made us stay away, saying it would be dangerous. Then while it was still a little dark and a bit misty they turned on the gas. One by one the gas was ignited at each intersection. Four or five foot yellow flames shot skyward out of each vent pipe all over town. It was like candles on a giant birthday cake. It wasn't long before the lines were clear and they turned off each intersection one by one. It was barely light out when it was all over. It's something you only see once in a lifetime and it was something.

Dad's Turtle

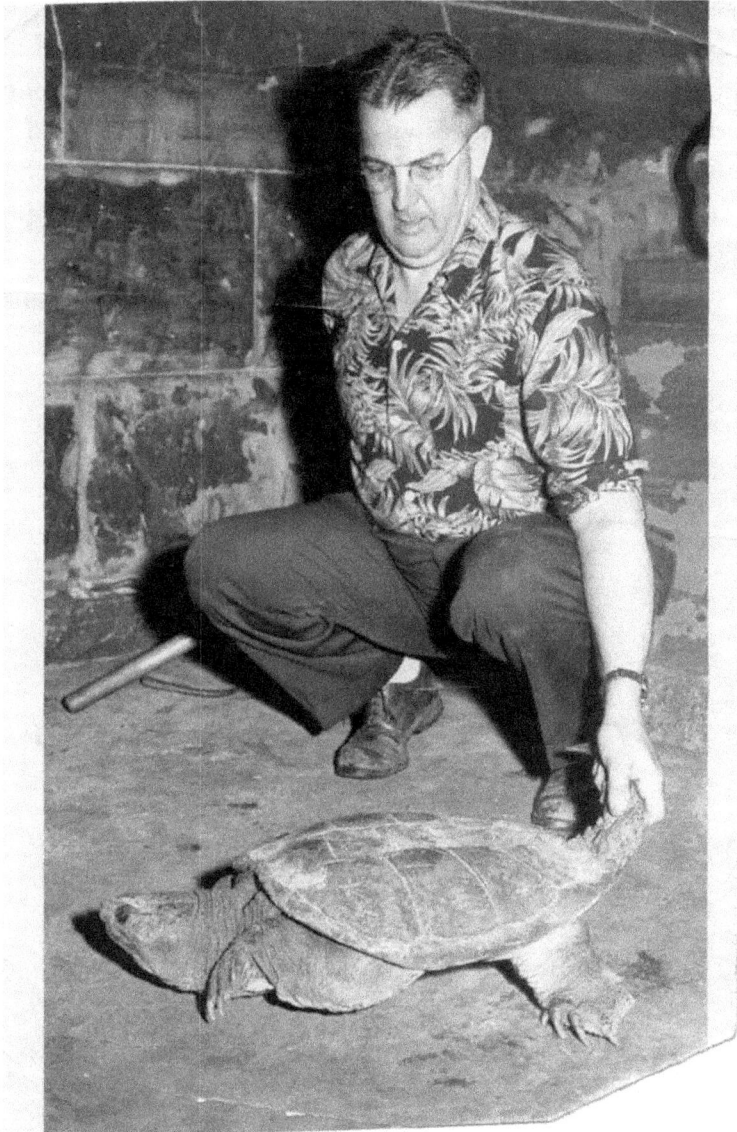

My Dad was out at camp when he saw a huge snapping turtle crossing the road and for some obscure reason he decided to capture it. Back home he took it from the trunk and put it in a bucket big enough to hold it. It was in the garage the next day when we kids put small sticks in front of it to watch it quickly snap them in half. At the time we had no clue we were doing anything wrong. No one knew about cruelty to animals, it was just a turtle. My Dad arranged to give it to a local restaurant in exchange for a free dinner with turtle soup. He even got his picture in the paper holding it, a picture he hung on the wall by his desk.

The White Birch Club

The White Birch Club was a hunting club formed by my father and seven of his friends when he was a young man. Most of the other members had moved away and only one other family used it besides ours. During hunting season my father was the de facto cook. Every summer we were obliged to go to the camp and cut firewood for the next hunting season. The first drive out in the spring was a job in itself. First we would stop at Newfoundland at a small gas station that sold ice. The owner always wore one of those gas station hats. Like a baseball cap without a beak. Brown in color with the name of some supplier or tire brand on it. We would pull up to the wooden ice house not much bigger than a garden shed. The door was a heavy wooden affair with a time worn latch. The capped attendant would grab the ice tongs and pull a 100 pound block out from the pile. He would measure off the sizes we needed for the various insulated boxes we had and stab at the ice two or three times with an ice pick until the slab broke off. He then grabbed it with the ice tongs and hosted it into our boxes. We got gas for the chain saws and for the old Willys Jeep my father had and off we went.

1977 Driveway to camp

The camp was at the end of a two mile dirt road only a few miles from Newfoundland. The first part of the dirt road was wide and well maintained as there were working farms that used it. Once past the last farm the road disappeared into the dense woods. If you did not know the road was there you would miss it. Once inside the woods we had to slow down as the road was very rutted. You could drive a car down the road once it was cleared but you had to ride the crest in the center or you would bottom out. The undergrowth closed in on the sides of the road the farther in we got. Sometimes we would stop and get out the chainsaw to clear a fallen tree. Often it took hours to make that first trip in the spring. There were places when the hills were so steep, the turns sharp and the road narrow I felt sure we were going over the edge. We never did.

I always looked forward to making the first sight of the camp through the woods and would holler out when I saw it. It was a big 30x30 foot two story cinder block building with a porch that went all across the front. Hung from the middle of the porch was a sign, "White Birch Club." If you thought the road to the camp was bad the driveway into the camp itself was even worse. It was as if they just marked a line through a rock field with little attempt to clear it. My father, who owned a tile store at one time, brought out tons of broken red asphalt tile to 'pave' the driveway. Over the years the tile had broken into little pieces. I never saw the driveway before this 'improvement' so I can only assume it was much worse then.

White Birch Club from the driveway.

Once past the rock pile the grounds were nice. (Well, nicer than this picture would make you think.) The driveway went around to the back where the kitchen door was at ground level with a small roofed porch of about 10x10 feet. There was a bench between the two roof support posts that we used to sit on while preparing food for dinner.

Yikes, you can see my underpants!

John and Bill, Jr., preparing for the evening meal.

The kitchen ran the entire length of the cabin and about one third of the width. As you went in there was a sink and cupboard on the right with an enormous picnic table that could sit 20 people or more that ran the entire length to the front. Then on the left a cupboard and a big wood stove and an oil burning heater. The ice box was at the front on the other side of the doorway from the oil heater. Through the door into the large great room that took up the rest of the ground floor was a huge fieldstone fireplace in the wall separating the great room from the kitchen. The ceiling beams were made from logs with a wooden floor above. At the back of the room was a pull down staircase that lead to the bunk room where everybody slept. In later years my father put a chunk stove in the fireplace for the winter. For springtime the fireplace was used.

The well, our water supply, a stone well, was over to the right as you went out the back door and about 50 feet away. It was a hand dug well with flagstone sides.

When I was a kid we would drop a bucket down the well and haul it up full of water. Sounds simple, doesn't it? If you just dropped the bucket down it would hit the water upright. You could jiggle the rope but that wouldn't work. You had to drop the bucket upside down, dead in the middle of the well. If it hit the side it would flip and usually land upright. It all boils down to technique, which of course, I never mastered. It took me several tries with half filled buckets to fill the one bucket I brought to the well to fill. We should have had one of those cranks you see in the movies with a wooden bucket on a rope. I guess the wooden bucket was heavy enough to just sink when it reached the water. A few years later we replaced the bucket on a rope with an old gas powered pump so I'll never know if that would have worked. The well was covered by a big lid that we were forever leaving open. This drove my father to distraction, he would yell at us in pure and utter frustration. My father never hit me although I thought he was going to on several occasions. However, my four brothers made up for that deficiency.

If you went to the left out the back door about 100 feet you ended up at the outhouse. An outhouse is a device designed to make you appreciate indoor plumbing. It is a hole in the ground with a shed over top it. A bench inside the shed had holes or if you were lucky an actual toilet seat upon which you did your business. There was a bucket of lime and a small shovel that you were supposed to put in afterwards to control the odor. I don't want to know how bad it would have been without the lime. As a kid we always wondered what was down there that might bite what we had hanging down through the hole so we never lingered long.

All Board and No Batten

My father wanted to build a shed at the camp the size of a two car garage. I don't remember what the original purpose of it but it ended up storing firewood. He had five sons which meant he had five critics on jobs like this. Phrases like "Christ Pop this will never work," were common. You had to be tough to be a Hogg in our family.

Tom running the dual trailer tractor trailer with Rich looking on in front of the shed we built. The addition on the right is the garage. Note the shed is full of firewood. The back door of the camp is just out of sight to the left.

The construction was to take place all on one weekend. Pop drove us hard, we resisted … as usual. We started by laying down large flat rocks in the four corners. Frost heave was not considered. On the rocks we set tree trunks of the appropriate length, braced by boards. Once the sides were up we put smaller logs across them to form the roof. Rough sawn boards were placed on those logs and roll roofing applied. For the side walls my father had procured wide green rough sawn boards from a local sawmill. We put these up vertically and he would yell at us to make sure they were tight. Almost every board wasn't tight enough for him. "Come on Frank push that tighter." He would yell. "Turn it the other way it will fit better." We pushed and tugged and struggled to make every joint as tight as we could. Finally at the end of the weekend we were done. Proud of our handiwork we went home to Scranton.

About a month later we came back to the camp for the weekend. When the new shed came into sight we boys started laughing so hard we were crying. All those green boards had shrunk at least an inch and the shed walls looked like a picket fence. My father, while embarrassed was undaunted and went back to the sawmill and bought enough 4 inch wide boards to cover the gaps. Now I know why they make board and batten siding. As we grew up we always made it a point to tell this story at family gatherings. My father was a good sport about it. With five sons pointing out his every faux pas, he had to be.

SHED BUILT ON TREES AT THE CAMP

We didn't know it at the time but my Dad's hobby turned out to be collecting firewood. He had far more than he could use but we didn't know that then because he was the only one who went to the camp in the winter to burn it. He was the self designated cook for the hunters who came out. I once asked him if he hunted himself. He had, after all, a large collection of hunting rifles.

"I used to hunt when I was a young man, go out in the woods, kill something and drag it back to camp. But that's a lot of work so now I just go out behind the camp a little ways and if a deer comes running by with enough momentum to carry him up on the porch, I'll shoot him." He said.

I have pictures of him with things he shot, a moose in Canada for example. So I know he did hunt at one time. I never did hunt myself but that's a story for another time.

Back at the camp my Pop had filled all the woodsheds he had with wood and wanted to make another. He had a spot for it too, right at the edge of the lawn out back were there were three trees in a perfect right angle. His plan was to use these three trees as the uprights for a shed. We kidded him by saying that as the trees grew the roof would go higher and higher.

"No, trees grow from the top and the roof would stay where it was forever." He said.

I didn't buy that but I knew small plants grew that way so I shut up and helped him build the shed. It only took a few hours. We had to add one vertical post and then nail joists to it and the three trees. Then cross rafters, boards and roofing and the job was done. He was right, that damn shed lasted for decades.

Every year Pop would shame us into going to the camp for a week or two to cut firewood. On the drive out he would scour the woods looking for fallen trees.

"That's a nice beech there and it looks like we can get the jeep close enough to drag it out." Would be the typical conversation. At dinner or lunch he would tell us about other candidates he found for us to, "Drag out."

The system we used was simple. We'd go out and trim all the small branches off the trunk and cut the trunk into manageable lengths. Sometimes we would cut the trunk into fireplace lengths. It depended on the circumstances.

Then all the smaller limbs would be gathered and hauled back for firewood for the kitchen stove.

Pop had a special sawhorse with the ends like an 'X' We put a shelf on the outside end to set the chainsaw on. I would run the saw while Pop fed the limbs in. It was an efficient way to cut the small stuff up.

All the split wood would be stacked bark side up because rain would run off it as the bark acted like a roof and kept the inner wood dry. I don't know if that really worked, it sounded reasonable so we did it. All the wood would be put in one of the designated sheds.

The first shed Pop built was very tall in front, 12 foot or so with a sloping flat roof that went down to 8 or 10 foot in back. It was as big as a two car garage. When he filled that up we added more roof to the back following the same pitch until the roof was only a few feet off the ground. Then he went sideways adding a shed about the size of a one car garage and it was really used for a garage and toolshed. Which by the way was the original reason for the big shed next to it that was now full of wood.

Many years later my brother Bruce, who still lived in Scranton, called all the brothers.

"I just came from the camp and the wood Pop has been collecting is starting to rot. He's cutting more wood than he's using so I told him we wouldn't help him cut any more until he burns up what he has." Bruce said. "We've all got to stick together on this."

It makes me feel kinda sad looking back on it. Cutting wood was Pop's hobby. If I had to do it over I would have suggested he sell some of the firewood to make room for more. I don't know if he could persuade any of us to help him cut more wood now that we knew it wasn't "for the hunting season"

I Don't Think I'm Going to Like What you Have to Tell Me

The last time I talked to him he was heading out for a business trip down near the camp. The camp itself was originally bought by 8 friends, Pop being one of them. Over the decades 6 of his friends died off and the ownership transferred to their sons. Those 6 never used the camp and didn't live anywhere near it. It was just Pop and the Crawford's that used it. The 6 got together and voted to sell it over Pop's objections and he didn't have the money to buy it himself. It must have hurt him more than he let on even though he said he was fine with it. He had a heart condition that he wasn't talking about and didn't have long to live and knew it. He asked me before his trip about some things that were at the camp. He was planning to stop by one last time to pick up a few things. He asked me if I wanted the vise that was bolted to the bench in the garage. I didn't really need it but I said yes and he said he would get it for me.

Pop was always going on sales trips. He would usually leave on Monday morning and come back Friday. Sometimes he would stay longer so no one was suspicious when he didn't come back that Friday. Pop had given the firewood he'd cut to some friends and they came out to the camp on Saturday to haul some of it away. They found Pop standing up behind the trunk of his car keeled over into it dead. At first they thought he was alive but when they got closer they realized he was dead. Pop died standing up which I think is kinda cool.

One of the most difficult things I ever had to do was tell my Mom. I got the call early Sunday but all the details weren't in. My brother Bruce was heading out to the camp and would call his son, my nephew Rich with those details. I waited, using the excuse that I wanted the details that Mom would want to know. In truth I needed to deal with it myself and work up the courage to tell her.

I knocked on her door and she was quite surprised to see me on a Sunday and happy too.

"Well, isn't this nice, what brings you over here?" She said. Then the look on my face and the fact she hadn't heard from Pop tipped her off.

"I don't think I'm going to like what you have to tell me." She said as she stood aside and let us in.

"I'm sorry Mom, Pop is dead, they found him at the camp." I said.

"What am I going to do, what am I going to do." She said again and again.

The rest of the day was a blur and the days after that too. Bruce had taken Pop's almost new car back to Scranton and cleaned out the trunk from whatever happens when a body is leaning into for the hot days in July before he was found. We don't know what day he died but his body was there for some days at least. Later Bruce drove the car up to Syracuse so I could sell it and give the money to Mom. Mom told me that Pop made sure the car loan would be paid off if he died and it almost killed the deal when they didn't want to do it. It was a way for Pop to get Mom another 10 grand because he couldn't get any more life insurance with his heart condition. People who work for themselves don't get the benefits others do. That's the down side, the up side is you can work half days whenever you want and you can pick which 12 hours that is too. That was a joke my father liked to tell.

Rich and I put together an obituary that really built him up. Saying he was the CEO of his own company, etc. We took that down to the Post Standard and gave it along with a very nice picture of Pop. The next day it was featured top and center with his picture really big like he was some hotshot rather than just a traveling salesman. We knew he would have liked that. The last joke he pulled on the world he left.

When I got the car from Bruce I had to unload all the stuff in it. There in a double brown paper bag was the vise Pop got for me. I don't know what triggered the last heart attack that killed him, I hope it wasn't the vise. But it was inevitable that it would happen sometime and what better place to die than at the camp he loved rather than while driving down the highway where he might have caused an accident that caused someone else to die.

Pop's body was taken to the local coroner who called me to ask what he should do with the remains. He suggested that the only thing that could be done was cremation for reasons I won't go into. Pop's body was there for an unknown amount of time and it was July. The coroner was eager to have something done soon. I didn't want to rush my mother and I wanted the decision to come from her so I put the coroner of for a day. He wasn't happy about that. By the next day my mom decided that cremation was the best thing to do and I called the coroner to give him the news.

The plan was that Bruce would bring the remains to Syracuse when he brought up Dad's car. In the meantime I was to get an urn for the remains. Pop was aways frugal and trying to get a good deal on things and I felt I owed it to him to do the same. I called around and found out the funeral directors had the urn market locked up and you had to buy it from them. I went to one and looked at urns and picked out a simple modest one that looked a bit like a shiney brass cigar box. I tried to get a break on the price which surprised the funeral director. I explained why but he wouldn't budge. He knew he had the market locked up and that I had to pay full price. He offered to transfer the ashes to the urn at no extra charge but I declined as I didn't think it a big deal. My opinion of funeral directors was not very high and future encounters with them hasn't changed that. Did you know you can buy a $4,000 casket from the funeral director or get the very same one for $1,400 from Amazon? Yup, it's true.

Bruce brought the ashes up to Syracuse in a black plastic box he got from the crematorium that was easily twice the size of the urn I bought. Hmm, I thought to myself. I wonder what the funeral director would do with the ashes that wouldn't fit in the urn… But I had a plan. I knew from my dental lab experience that vibration would pack the ashes tighter in the urn. I started filling the urn with the grey gritty ashes and gently tapped the urn with a small hammer. It took about a half hour but I got every bit of ash in the urn. Using a scratch awl I scratched a brief message on the inside of the lid and went to install it with the one way screws provided that would prevent the box from being opened once sealed. At that point I realized the lid did not provide a water tight seal and once buried in the ground water could seep in. I was doing this in my workshop late at night. I knew I had some silicon somewhere and set off to find it. All I could find was automotive orange high heat silicone. The high heat type was of higher quality that ordinary silicone so it was a good choice.

I applied the silicone and sealed up the urn, wiped off the excess and it was done. All the time I was doing this, the tapping of the ashes and everything else I was talking to Pop, telling him what I was doing and why. When I scratched the writing on the inside of the lid I read it to him and told him I loved him. Then when it was all sealed up with the high heat silicone I told Pop about it and said, "I don't know which way you're going Pop, up or done, but this will protect you either way."

Some time later we took Pop's urn to Union PA and buried him in the cemetery at the Union Church, which houses many of our family members.

While we were in the area my mother and I ordered a head stone with both their names on it and they installed it some time later. They spelled my mother's name with an 'i' instead of an 'e' and she didn't want to change it. I can truthfully say that I'm not happy having a tombstone at the Union Church in Union PA with my name on it.

July 23, 1987

.linsky

Bernice Salinsky,
·ence St., Brewer-
Tuesday at St.
.al, will be at 8:45
: Williams Funeral
1. in Sacred Heart
Cicero. Burial will
: Cemetery, Clay.
are 2 to 4 and 7 to 9
the funeral home,

Herkimer, Mrs.
ved in Brewerton
vas a communicant
rt Church and a
Altar and Rosary

her husband, John;
Erieville; and a

may be made to
nteer Fire Depart-
verton Ambulance

lillbyer

lillbyer, 68, of 178
·e died Wednesday
lospital.
was a life resident
le was a self-em-
inter.
vas a Navy veteran
II and the Korean

e his wife, Kath-
: Rev. Terrance of
vo stepdaughters,
dt of Cape Coral,
3americk of Syra-
Harold G. Capace
grandchildren and
andchildren.
he at 10·30 a m

William T.M. Hogg, 84;
ran manufacturer's agency

Memorial services for William
T.M. Hogg, 84, of 124 Lincoln Park
Drive, who died last Thursday in
Pike County, Pa., will be at 7 p.m.
today in University United Methodist Church.
The family will receive friends at
the church after the services.
Mr. Hogg was chairman of Wm.
T.M. Hogg Co., a manufacturer's
agency which represented ETC
Inc. and Scot Laboratories, as well
as other suppliers of industrial
chemicals.
At the time of his death, Mr.
Hogg was returning from a business trip in Newburgh when he
stopped at his hunting club in Pike
County. It was there that he died
unexpectedly.
Mr. Hogg was a native of Philadelphia, Pa. From 1935 to 1953 he
operated Lackawanna Linoleum
Store in Scranton, Pa. Mr. Hogg
continued in the floor covering
business when he moved to Syracuse in 1958, and his operation
evolved into a manufacturer's
agency.
Mr. Hogg was a member of University United Methodist Church
and the International Sanitary
Supply Association. He was a 32nd-
degree Mason of Union Lodge,
Scranton, and Irem Shrine Temple
in Wilkes-Barre, Pa. He was an
affiliate member of Tigris Shrine
Temple.
Surviving are his wife, the for-

WILLIAM T.M. HOGG

mer Frances E. Kelley; five sons,
William T.M. Hoag of Malvern, Pa.,
Bruce K. Hogg of Scranton, John
E. Hogg of Hamilton, Va., C.
Thomas Hogg of Louisville, Ky.,
and Frank T. Hogg of Syracuse; a
sister, Joanna Ruhl of Lancaster,
Pa.; a brother, Joseph of West
Grove, Pa.; seven grandchildren
and several nieces and nephews.
Contributions may be made to
the Shriners' Crippled Children's
Hospital.

I still have that vise and it's still in the double brown
paper bag. I never took it out, not once and I never will.
Right now it sets up in the attic. Every now and then I take
a look inside as if I'm going to see something that isn't
there. Maybe one day I will take it out, maybe I'll put it on
my workbench and actually use it. That would make more
sense than leaving it in that bag. I was going to say that vise
has a hold on me but that's just too corny.

Camp Tales

The outhouse is to the left, the woodshed is center and the camp is behind the tree on the right.

One time my brother Bruce, a Ham radio operator, rigged a device with a 9 volt battery, a buzzer, some parts and some wire. If you were holding these two wires when he pushed the button you got quite a shock, nothing that would hurt you. But it would give you quite a start. Tom and I took this out to the outhouse. I rigged the two wires around the back of the toilet seat everyone used and hid the ends in among the chipped paint of the seat. The second toilet was pretty bad so everyone used this one.

We waited…

My father turned out to be our first 'victim.' We waited until he was settled in and sneaked up behind the outhouse and pushed the button…

"JESUS!" we heard him say and we heard him get up off the seat.

We waited… By the sounds coming from inside it seemed he had settled in to the seat, so we hit the button again.

"SON OF A BITCH!" He said and again we heard him get up from the seat.

We waited for a while and we didn't hear any noise so we hit the button again. Nothing, we waited a bit then hit it again … nothing. We quietly sneaked around the side of the building and there was my father, bent over, hands on his knees, pants down around his ankles, peering back into the outhouse, trying to see what got him. He spotted us and knew immediately it was us. He couldn't chase us with his pants around his ankles so he just cursed us out.

However, he had us rig it so that he could operate it from the cabin during hunting season.

On another occasion we rigged a speaker underneath the outhouse and when a woman would go into the outhouse we would say. "Would you mind moving over lady, I'm painting down here."

TO BB OR NOT TO BB

On one of the trips out to the camp when I was about 10 my father was acting a bit smug, something was up but I didn't have a clue. Once at the camp my father dragged out

71

this long thin cardboard box with DAISY clearly printed on the cover. It was a BB gun and it was for me! My own gun! I carefully read the instructions and loaded the BB's into it. It was night so I had to wait till the next day to try it out.

My first live target was a chipmunk. I stalked the little guy for what seemed like hours till he sat still on a fallen log. I fired and he fell off the back of the log. I ran over and there his body lay on the ground, dead. No longer the cute creature of just a moment ago, now a lifeless piece of fur and meat. The feeling of elation was gone, replaced by sadness. I covered him with some leaves and dirt and decided to try my hand at birds.

Birds are very hard to shoot with a BB gun. I had a great time trying though. For most of the day I fired at birds never hitting one of them. Then in mid afternoon I hit a small bird and he came tumbling down from his perch and landed just a few feet in front of me on the path. I went over to him and he lay there with his left wing broken about halfway out. He was flapping and crying, partly in pain, partly in fear. He cried and looked at me. I didn't know what to do. I ran back to the camp and told my brother Tom what had happened. He told me that I had to put the bird out of its misery, I had to go back and kill it. I ran back to the woods, the bird still there, still crying. I took my gun and aimed, tears welling up in my eyes, I missed. I tried again … missed, fired again … missed. Again and again I tried to kill the little helpless bird. Tears running down my face clouding my vision. I took aim, closed my eyes … missed. The poor bird was scared out of its wits and in pain and I couldn't do the right thing.

I ran back to get Tom who was disgusted with me but he came to the bird, took my gun, aimed and with one shot killed it. He turned and walked past me on the path, handed me my gun and muttered 'sissy.' Full of remorse I dug a grave and buried the little bird.

It's over 40 years later and in my mind I can still see that bird. I was never much of a hunter after that.

APPLE TREES AND TREE FORTS

The apple trees at the camp played a major role in our families' photo history, especially the one directly in front of the cabin. The main trunk grew at a 45 degree angle and was perfect for climbing. Pictures of my brothers and me on that tree sprinkle our history. It was always there and lives on in my memory. I've never gone to see what happened to the camp after my Dad died. I know the new owners tore the cabin down and probably cut the trees down too. That is something I don't need to see. I want my memory of the camp what it was, not what it is. With Dad gone, so too is the camp gone. He was the camp and without him the rest is just debris that mars the idyllic memory of the good times I had there as a kid.

SAME TREE, DIFFERENT KIDS

The tree in the picture on the previous page, the one to the left growing at a 45 degree angle is an apple tree. There were many apple trees at the camp but this one was special. Probably because it was just a few feet from the front porch which is just to the left. More likely because it was very easy to climb. It was there when I was a kid and it was there the last time I was at the camp. I'd like to believe that tree is still there, waiting silently for the day the kids come back to play all over it.

We nailed boards to it and made tree houses on it and every year it was there waiting for us. Not just me but every kid in our family. The following pictures are a memorial to that tree.

63

64

Yikes, you can see my underpants!

1967

Yikes, you can see my underpants!

TOM SHOT ME!

It was at the camp where my brother Tom shot me with his BB gun. We were situated about 20 feet apart each behind an old piece of plywood taking turns shooting. First I would stand up and fire at his plywood and duck down and it would be his turn. This one time, in a shot of pure chance, Tom's, BB hit the barrel of my gun, which was sticking up and ricocheted off it and hit me. Now a BB likely won't kill you but it sure can sting.

I let out a yell,

"You shot me, you shot me, you did it on purpose, look you can see the dent your BB made on the barrel of my gun!" I yelled.

Tom protested that it was a fluke, that he couldn't have done that if he tried and he didn't try. But I, the injured one, wasn't going to let him off that easy.

"You did it on purpose, you tried to KILL me." I said.

"No, I didn't and you know it," he said.

At this point I went to my father with the hope that he would punish Tom.

"What the hell were you two doing shooting at each other anyway, you're lucky you didn't put an eye out." Pop said.

And then he took both our BB guns away.

"See, see" Tom said, "You opened your big mouth and now neither of us can shoot our guns."

"You did it on purpose." I muttered under my breath, chagrined that my plan failed so miserably.

"You did it on purpose." I muttered again, dejected as I followed him out the door.

The Strange Mind of an 11 Year Old

When I was 11 or so Nay Aug park had a very large man made swimming lake, the largest I've ever seen. It had a concrete bottom and large pipes all around pumping the filtered water back into the lake. The end of the pipes were above the waterline. You could have a lot of fun playing in front of the water coming out of those pipes. But even with that we still liked to swim in Roaring Brook just behind Nay Aug park at a place now called Nay Aug Gorge.

Back then we just called it, "The Falls." There is a tree house overlooking the gorge now with walkways of wood throughout the area. They have taken advantage of the uniqueness of it and it is displayed prominently on their web site. Tourism, plain and simple. Back when I was a kid the only place you could see the 'gorge' was from the old trestle bridge that was closed off to car traffic. We had to walk down a long path through the woods to get to it. You couldn't see it from the park. It was forbidden to swim there but that just made it better.

One swim area we liked was at the bottom of the gorge that erosion had created over eons of time. You could dive in from the side perhaps 20 feet and then climb back up and do it again. The climb was tricky, the rocks slippery and often you would slip and fall back in. Every year kids would get hurt or killed doing just that.

One warm summer day we were walking down the path to the falls with our swimsuits rolled in our towels. We met several firemen coming up the path from the falls, carrying a stretcher between then with a body covered by a blanket. We moved off to the side of the path to let them pass. When they got to us they stopped and one of the firemen lifted the blanket to show us the body of a young boy about our age. He was gray and lifeless. I don't remember what the fireman said, something about the danger of the falls I guess. They covered the boy back up and we watched the backs of the firemen as they carried him up the path until they were out of sight.

Then we got back on the path and went swimming at the falls.

Like you, I wonder now what could have been going on in my mind. Didn't I see or understand the danger or was it that the mind of an 11 year old can't comprehend the danger or think that he could die. I vote for the latter as this wasn't the first dumb thing I did.

TRAIN HOPPING

The fastest way to get to one of our swimming holes was to hop a train. As they left the yards at downtown Scranton they moved slowly up the long hill to the swimming hole. The scene you see in the movies of people jumping into empty box cars is pure fiction. They close the doors and even if they were open the floor of the boxcar is shoulder height and there is nothing under it to latch onto. It is like jumping onto a diving board from the side. It just isn't done. You would need a ladder to get into it if the train was stopped. They weren't stopped where we jumped on and although they were moving slow they were still moving.

You could grab any ladder on the side of any of the cars, they all had them, but the ladder on boxcars went to the top and therefore boxcars were the best to hop. They weren't the best to ride as it is very tiring to hang onto the side of the boxcar and the conductor in the caboose might see you. Riding between boxcars isn't much better. There is a ladder there too. The best way to ride was to hop a boxcar just before or after a tanker. Once on the train you would climb over to the tank car and sit on the turret walkway with your back leaning up against the turret. The reason you got on the boxcar rather than directly on the tank car is because the ladder on the tank car only goes up a few steps and it's hard to grab onto. If you couldn't find a tank car, a flatcar is the next best choice.

Riding a boxcar is not fun as you have to hang out the side or between the cars. Riding the top is okay but we had to go through one tunnel just before the swimming hole and riding on the top through a tunnel is scary and breathing diesel fumes isn't fun. I know, I did it, but just once. I lay on my back and coughed at the fumes and watched the rocky ceiling of the tunnel which seemed to be just inches away. It scared the crap out of me.

Eventually you'll have to get off the train and it's starting to gain speed by the time we exited the tunnel near our swimming hole There is a technique to doing it and it isn't what you see in the movies where the actor makes this giant leap into the tall grass on the side of the tracks. There is a lot of crap, big rocks, old railroad ties, appliances, you name it, on the sides of the track by a railroad and jumping blindly into that is just plain stupid. That's done only in the movies.

When it comes time to jump off you climb back onto the boxcars outer ladder with your foot on the bottom rung and your hand down low so if you were standing next to the train your hand would be holding the rung about shoulder high. With your hand on the ladder step down and start to run with giant steps until you are sure you're not going to trip and end up under the train, then you let go of the ladder while you simultaneously turn away from the train as you slow down.

If you are a 12 year old boy this seems like a perfectly reasonable way to travel.

One day we decided to see where the train went after the swimming hole so we stayed on. The train picked up speed and we all moved to a flatcar with sides that was loaded with iron ingots each weighing about 30-50 pounds. After a bit we got bored and decided to throw some of the ingots over the side. They made an impressive impact with the ground so we decided to hit a tree with one. We almost emptied the entire load and never even came close to hitting a tree. It didn't look like the train was ever going to slow down and we were pretty far from town so we decided to jump off. One by one we jumped. When my turn came I tried to do giant steps but when I let go of the ladder I couldn't do more than 2 or 3 steps before I tumbled and rolled uncontrollably. First I rolled away from the wheels then I rolled back, my head hit some part of the wheel assembly, maybe the wheel itself and I rolled away from the train. In my minds eye to this day I can see that train wheel just inches from my head. I ended up with a small gash on my forehead just over my left eye.

We gathered together and went back down the tracks looking for the other boys. The last boy was over the side of an embankment laying sprawled on the rocks below. We thought he was dead, but he was playing a joke on us. We walked back to town waiting for a freight to jump, none came but we did see two engines coming at full speed and we realized that we couldn't jump a train going that fast anyway. We got back well after dark after walking for perhaps 6 hours. We all got hell for being late but that didn't stop us from jumping trains.

My parents never asked if we were hopping trains, perhaps they thought we were too smart to do such a stupid thing. I didn't think much of it. It was just an easy way to get from my house to Nay Aug park and we did it regularly, perhaps 4-5 times a week. It was just part of our life, normal everyday stuff.

KID POOPING IN HIS PANTS

About five of us were walking down a well worn path above Roaring Brook when one boy said he had to take a poop. A tree nearby was perfect with a low branch only a foot or so above the ground. After he pooped the next boy went but not close to the trunk in the same place as the first boy, but further out. As each boy went he moved further out the branch which got higher each time. For some reason no boy wanted to poop on top of another boys poop. The last boy to go was also the shortest and the branch too high for his feet to touch the ground. With his pants at his ankles, he had to swing his feet under him to keep his balance. Yep, he took a dump right into his pants. No one headed his pleas for help cleaning the poop from his pants and he had to follow behind as we wouldn't let him walk with us on the way home.

THE DUMB KID

It seems that every neighborhood has a dumb kid. Ours was a big loaf of a kid. You could go up to him and ask him quick for two dimes for a nickel and he would give it to you. I sold him a piece of shinny lead once by telling him it was silver. One day I went to his house to sell him something and his mother answered the door. She thanked me for being friends with her son as no one else would, because he was slow. That taught me a lesson I'll never forget. Everybody has feelings, everybody deserves to live a happy life and my taking advantage of his slowness was just plain wrong. I never took advantage of him again after that. I spent time with him and learned that although he was slow he wasn't stupid, you just had to be patient.

It amazes me to this day how kids can be so mean and hate those who are different from them, just because they are different. It seems that has changed in the years hence. It took a mother thanking me for something I didn't do, with the kindness she thought I had, to make an impression on me. George Bernard Shaw was right when he said: *Youth is a wonderful thing; too bad it's wasted on the young.* With life comes experience and with experience we grow and become better people. I learned a valuable lesson that day, one that I carry with me always.

STEALING ICE CREAM

On one end of Nay Aug Lake was a concession stand. They sold all kinds of junk, cheap bamboo canes, balloons, ice cream bars and other stuff. One day I noticed that a small broken window had just been replaced and I got an idea. I told my friends that we could remove that new pane of glass and they could climb in and rob the place leaving by the door while I replaced the pane of glass. We did just that but there wasn't much worth stealing. We took cases of ice cream bars over to the picnic area. Most of the ice cream melted but they never figured out how we broke in until now. I didn't do it because I wanted to break into the place, I did it because I wanted to see if we could get away with it. I spent a lot of time putting that window pane back in and smoothing the putty down, more time then my buddies took robbing the place. Even then I took pride in doing a job well and I wanted more than anything to get away with it.

The next day we wandered by the stand and I noticed that no one realized how we got in. No one was looking at the replaced pane and I was pleased to see that I did a good job on it, even in the dark.

They found the boxes of melted ice cream bars in the picnic area but they never found out who did it.

FART LIGHTING

In any good childhood there is one really gullible kid. In my case it was my next door neighbor Billy's kid brother. We bet him that he could not light a fart. After some cajoling he dropped his pants, lifted his legs and we all waited with a match at the ready for the moment. The kid brother said NOW and we lit the match, he farted, a blue flame erupted from his anus and he screamed. Clutching his butt he ran, pants down around his ankles, to his back door, where his mother had come to see what the commotion was all about. We all ran off in different directions so I don't know the final outcome. After that we couldn't talk that kid into anything.

TOM'S GIRLFRIEND

My brother Tom is 2 years older than me to the day. Sharing birthdays with him was not my idea. Being older than I, he was the first to discover that girls were neat to play with. One day, or evening he was 'playing' with his girlfriend on the other side of the hedge while I waited impatiently on the sidewalk. To our dismay the girls father did not like Tom and was hiding in the bushes waiting to catch him 'playing' with his daughter. I discovered this when Tom came running past me with the father in hot pursuit. It was at that moment that I discovered I could run much faster than Tom.

The father couldn't run as fast as either of us and we got away clean.

HURRICANE HAZEL AND THE KID WITH ALL THE TOYS

One day one of my older brothers took me down to meet a new kid my age. He had just about every toy you could think of. He had a big hook and ladder fire engine truck that I particularly liked but he was selfish and wouldn't let me play with his stuff. After a bit I left thinking he was the luckiest kid around. I found out later that his father had drowned in the hurricane caused flood that hit Scranton and his uncles bought him all those toys.

This was another experience that helped shape my life. Sometimes what you think you see, isn't what you see at all. What I thought was a selfish kid was a kid grieving over his lost Dad. These little lessons, these experiences are what we are made of, what we become is what we experience as a kid. The right experience makes us better. Who knows what causes bad people to be bad but I'd bet it started when they were very young.

The Step Falls

Just up Roaring Brook from the Harrison Avenue bridge are the Step Falls. You can see them from the bridge. You can even see them from Google Earth. I call them the Step Falls because the way they were made, they looked like steps. Heavy rectangular slabs of rock, probably 2 foot by 4 foot rise up from the floor of the Brook for perhaps 30 feet. It almost looks like a dam but there is fill behind the rocks so it isn't a dam. My guess is that it was done to slow the speed of the brook to prevent erosion at the bridge. After all it is called Roaring Brook and it doesn't roar anymore.

These large rocks fit in a V notch between the granite sides of the stream bed and between the steps and the rock sides you have many places to dive into the pool below the falls. The water does not crash down to the bottom but rather flows from step to step in its gentle travel to the bottom. Because of this the water in the pool is only about 4 foot deep and has a cobblestone bottom. Diving into this from any height requires a special technique. You put your hands out like a regular dive but as soon as you hit the water you spread them out to cushion the shock of hitting the bottom. Twelve to fifteen feet seemed to be the highest you could go without hurting yourself. Most of the time we dived from the left side as you faced downstream because the rocks flattened out at the 12 foot mark to make a good spot to dive from. Diving from the steps themselves was very tricky as they were only about 4 or 5 inches wide and very slippery. If you fell you would bounce down them like a clown in the movies going down a flight of stairs.

We didn't swim there as much as a spot further up the Brook that was created during the flood of 1958. In that flood large concrete slabs that formed a retaining wall for the railroad tracks were washed into the creek bed at all different angles forming pools and diversions of the brook. One of them was at an angle that made it like a beach. It went into the water up to about 2 feet deep and then a drop-off to about 6 or 8 feet deep. The water ran slow and clear, so clear you could see right to the bottom. Once you dove in you could swim underwater up under the slabs if you had the courage.

Farther upstream was a place where the water was forced between two large rocks and were smoothed by time into an almost perfect water slide. However it was kind of scary as you were carried down very fast and totally out of control. I can only remember doing it once or twice.

The most used swimming hole was the one on the other side of the tunnel. It wasn't a swimming hole really, unless you screwed up. It was some kind of flood control system. There was a stream that led into Roaring Brook that was diverted through a concrete channel on the backside of a very large concrete pool, something like a swimming pool. I guess that with a lot of water the larger concrete swimming pool would hold the water temporally. It was never full when we were there, just about 1 to 2 feet of water with most of that muck, broken branches and who knows what else lurked in the muck. The total depth was about 4 feet. Along the side nearest the tracks was a large oak tree with a huge branch the hung over the center of the pool to which someone had hung a 2 inch thick rope with a big knot on the bottom. The knot was about a foot above the water.

Someone volunteered or got elected to wade through the muck to get the rope and bring it to the side by the tree. The trick was to grab the rope and run with it along the side as fast as you could and then swing in a big circle back to where you started. If you got enough speed you made it all the way around and kept your feet dry. If you got a really good swing you might try 2 circuits but if you didn't make it, you had to withstand the jeers of you pals and the unpleasant task of walking back through the muck.

We never hopped a train going home, back down the tracks. There were very few of them, but the few that did were going too fast because it was going downhill. We had to go through the tunnel to get back to Nay Aug park and back down Linden Street to get home. The tunnel and the short bridge over Roaring Brook are visible from satellite pictures of the area.

SLIDING ACROSS THE THIN ICE ON ROARING BROOK

In winter Roaring Brook is beautiful. The water that seeped out from the cliffs along the sides makes huge icicles like waterfalls frozen in time. The Brook itself was frozen on that day and we would get a running start on the banks where we had footing and slide across the ice at an angle to the other side. Back and forth we went running and sliding. Downstream from the single track bridge, a drainage pipe emptied into the brook. The water from the pipe was warmer and you could see its path into and down the brook by the thin black ice that was partially melted from the warmer water. I didn't know this at the time and as we ran and slid down the creek we didn't notice it until it was too late.

I took a run and started sliding across the ice when I saw the black ice. It was so thin you could see the water rushing under it. I was helpless, I couldn't stop, I yelled to my friend not to follow and watched in fascination as I slid to what I was sure was at best going to be a very cold swim. I hit the black ice and I could see it breaking under my feet but in a flash I was over it and unto the thicker white ice … safe! I looked back and there was water where I had just been. The ice was only cardboard thin. My momentum had saved me. As you read this book you're going to wonder, as do I, how I managed to survive this long. I guess it was just dumb luck with the emphasis on the dumb part.

WALKING UNDER THE TRESTLE

Just before the tunnel that goes to the rope swing is a trestle that was built after the flood of 1957. Each of the two tracks has its own bridge but it looks like one from the outside. Each bridge is made up of 2 huge I beams each about 5 foot high. The beams are braced by smaller angle iron about 3 inches wide. We got the idea to cross the trestle underneath the tracks. Just another in a long list of dumb ideas. The trestle is about 80 foot above the creek bed below and the bracing is far apart. Once we got under the tracks it seemed like a good idea. As we moved out into the center of the bridge the ground dropped away and it got very scary. The cross braces were about 6 feet apart and there wasn't much to hold onto as you went from one to the next. It would have been a disaster if a train came along while we were under there. As we walked we knocked small rocks loose from the flat areas of the metalwork and you couldn't help but watch them as they fell down into the water below. We finally made it across and professed our bravado to each other but none of us ever suggested we do that again.

Spike's Wire Clothesline and the Cop

I had a small dog with two spots, one on his butt and one on his head. At first I called him 'Two Spot' but that seemed stupid. After a while I changed that to 'Spike' like dogs were supposed to be called. 'Spike' did not live up to the vision of a dog most people think of when they hear the name 'Spike' He would bark loudly when a stranger came to the door but only after someone came into the room he knew. I guess he was waiting for backup before he spoke. Still he was my dog and I loved him. In the backyard my brother Bruce rigged a piece of heavy wire next to the clothesline with a ring to hook Spike's leash so he could have the run of the yard.

The neighbors on both sides had dogs, big dogs that must have influenced Spikes behavior. One winter I built a snow castle with a ramp for Spike to climb on. The first time he got to the top he just sat there and howled and barked. He sure showed those other dogs that day. He was king of the hill, the big dog at last.

One night I was in the living room reading and Spike was in the kitchen tied to the spot next to the back door where he lived. (My mother would not let him have the run of the house.) Unknown to me my brother Tom and his friend had gone downtown and gotten a stash of snow to make snowballs to throw at cars. One of the cars they targeted was owned by a very large policeman with huge eyebrows that did not appreciate their actions. Earlier that day my father had us move some junk from the basement to the back alley to the garage. We put a plank from the sidewalk up the two steps to the alley in the small space between our garage and our neighbors. We used that to run the wheel barrow on. The junk was piled in the garage. When we finished we just moved the plank to the side. It did not occur to us to bring in the empty ash cans while we had the wheelbarrow so we left them there at the top of the steps.

While reading in the living room I did not hear the light footsteps of my brothers friend as he ran between our house and the neighbors. I did not see him duck under

Spike's wire nor did I see him as he ran between the garages to the left of the plant and jump over the ash cans. I did hear the heavy footsteps of the cop running between the houses and the loud TWANG as he hit Spikes wire followed by the sound of footsteps, one on the sidewalk between the garages, one on the plank, sidewalk, plank, sidewalk... I then heard the CRASHING sound when he hit the ash cans.

I was standing up in the living room wondering what that noise was about when my brother crashed through the front door, threw his fleece lined coat on the radiator and rushed upstairs. I went over and tucked the coat into the radiator fins to hurry the process of warming it up. A few minutes later came a pounding at the back door. When I got to the kitchen Spike was facing the door as far from it as his leash would allow. When he saw me he started barking loudly. My father came down and answered the door. All I remember of it was that the cops huge eyebrows were standing straight out, I couldn't take my eyes off them. My father stood up for my brother and defended him. I brought out the fleece lined coat to show it was warm. After many angry words the cop left, a very unhappy man.

I don't know if Tom learned a lesson from all that, probably not, but it sure makes a good story to tell.

A Train in the Tunnel

Along Roaring Brook just below the Harrison Street bridge and below the step falls was a little used train tunnel. When I was about 12 we often tried to check out the length of that tunnel but it was so long, we never found the end.

One day we came across a rail car, you know one of those things the rail workers use to carry their tools. We took, well, stole the car and decided to use it to explore the tunnel. We made up torches from Sumac trees and took other tools and whatever else we thought we would need. Now before I go any further I must tell you I never saw a train use that tunnel, none of us did so we felt very confident that no train would be using it that day.

We started in the tunnel which curved gently to the right and soon we could not see any daylight behind us, it was very dark and we were scared. None of us would admit it so we carried on, lighting one torch after the other. After a very long time one of us said he heard something and we all stopped and held our breath. After a few minutes we saw a dim light flickering on the wet sides of the tunnel ahead and the unmistakable sound of a diesel engine coming through the tunnel. We had to take the rail car with us because if we just left it the train would crash and might kill us too. We gave it everything we had and managed to get the railcar out of the tunnel before the train came. In the middle of the bridge across Roaring Brook we decided we could no longer keep ahead of the train and we pushed the car over the side into the water just as the train was coming out of the tunnel. We jumped to the shore and waved at the engineer as they went by. They never saw the rail car.

Harrison Ave. Viaduct, Scranton, Pa.

In it's heyday things looked pretty good. The tunnel was deteriorating and rarely used.

Often when we wanted to hop a train there was none to hop. So we walked along the tracks to our destination. Like boys everywhere we talked about everything imaginable. I remember the sights and smells along the way. Railroads tracks have a distinctive smell of some combination of oil, grease, and diesel smoke and fuel. The tracks, ties and even the gravel all have a coating of brown/black crud. We would walk on the track itself or from tie to tie as the gravel (called ballast by railroad experts) is large and not comfortable on your feet. Today the track itself is all welded into one piece to avoid the clackety clack noise but back then they were bolted together with large plates. They also had a heavy flexible cable that went around the joint to assure electrical continuity. The ties were interesting as they were all different colors and age. When the railroad replaced ties they would usually replace a whole bunch at a time so you would see 5 or ten ties that looked the same age followed by a variety of ages.

We always looked for stuff between the tracks believing that something valuable might have fallen off a train. Sometimes we would put a penny on the track and get it the next day. Once a train runs over it becomes a long thin elliptical shape. Every now and then is a call box, always locked that the train workers could use to call the office (I guess).

Walking through the tunnel between the trestle and the rope swing was dicey. While the tunnel was only one or two blocks long a train could come along and trap you in there. The procedure was to hug the wall till it passed. While it seemed that there was enough room to continue walking next to the train we didn't. Sometimes you would see a boxcar with a bad wheel rocking back and forth as it came towards you. Besides the noise and threat of death was the thick smell of diesel smoke from the engine. It took quite some time for the smell to dissipate.

We could have used the other unused tunnel, the one that was abandoned after the flood, but what fun is that. Besides that tunnel felt creepy and we didn't like walking through it.

One time we found an old shoe by the tracks and we put in on the track, climbed the embankment and waited on a rock ledge to see how a train would crush it. Some time later a diesel running without cars came up the tracks slowly and stopped a few feet from the shoe. The engineer looked up at us and told us that that shoe could derail a train and asked us to come down and remove it. He was nice about it and we came down and took it off the tracks. Lesson learned, nuff said.

I Fought the Cab and the Cab Won

I've done a number of stupid things in my life and this has to rank right at the top. It's kinda weird how it came about. A bunch of us were riding our bikes near my old Taylor Street house where there is a big hill. We lived on Irving Ave at the time, which wasn't far from the bottom of the hill. It was a steep hill, a very steep hill. I visited it again just a few years ago and wondered what made me do that very stupid thing.

I bet my friends that I could ride down the hill and make the turn without using my brakes. This was not possible and I knew it but something made me do it anyway. I might have made it too if the Taxi Cab wasn't there. I ran head on into the cab and broke my left leg at the thigh. Didn't do my bike any good either. I lay there on the ground, kinda sitting, screaming, "Don't touch me" "Don't touch me!" and held my leg by the knee. Like all pain I don't remember how it felt, all I remember is that it really hurt. A nurse stopped by and offered help but I wouldn't let her touch me, "Don't touch me." I just screamed and screamed.

Soon the ambulance came and the pain must have made me pass out because the next thing I remember was being in the Emergency Room at Hahnemann Hospital. They said that they were going to give me something that would make the pain go away and soon I was dreaming of falling down an endless hole. At one point I could see myself laying on the table as if I were on the ceiling.

One of the neighborhood kids ran and told my Mom I was in a wreck but she arrived at the scene after they took me to the hospital. I was in the O.R. when she came so I didn't see her until after. But she looked in on me and okayed the procedure.

When I awoke I was in my hospital bed in traction. That wasn't pleasant. A stainless steel pin had been driven through my thigh bone just above my knee and was hooked to a big U shaped clamp which connected to a rope through a pulley to a heavy weight that pulled constantly on my leg. My leg was in a sling kind of thing with a ring near my crotch so the weight wouldn't pull me down the bed but would pull the lower part of my leg from the upper part. The bones were overlapped and this contraption was supposed to pull them back into line. Apparently the muscles contract and prevent this otherwise. I couldn't sleep for days because everytime I started to doze off my leg muscles would relax causing a searing pain which woke me right up.

As if that wasn't bad enough they were worried that I might get pneumonia so they brought in this evil device that was connected to an oxygen tank. Every fifteen minutes or so the nurse would come in and strap the mask on my face and turn the damn thing on. As soon as I started to take a breath this thing would blast a shot of cold oxygen into my lungs filling them right up. Five minutes of that and I was wide awake. Five minutes later she was back so I never could fall asleep after one of those. Desperate I studied the device and noticed a switch labeled, "Automatic" along with others that controlled duration, etc. After the nurse left I played around with them and found I could set it on automatic and it would breathe all by itself. I just let my mouth open and let it do it's thing. It woke me up every time but because it wasn't filling my lungs I could get back to sleep after she came and turned it off. But I was awake enough to turn off the automatic switch when she came back in the room because the machine blocked her view of what I was doing. I didn't mind it during the day but at night I had to get some sleep.

Like every red blooded 12 year old I got a crush on one of my nurses. She had short dark hair and oh was she pretty. I took a few pictures of her with my little blue and white camera my sister in law Janet brought me. Janet also brought me clay and crafts to play with and visited often.

My Mom would come to visit every day about lunchtime. I hated to see her go and I would hold myself up by the trampoline attached to the traction structure on my bed. After a few weeks of this I was able to hold myself up indefinitely. I did that when they came to change the sheets. I was reading a book one time and didn't realize they were done so I just kept holding myself up and reading. It didn't bother me a bit. When the nurse came in many minutes later she was all upset I was still up in the air despite my reassurances that it wasn't a problem. My upper body and abdominal strength is something I can only dream about these days but I bet I had a nice six pack back then.

I shared my room with three other beds with mine being by the window that looked out on the alley. Seniority I guess as I was there six weeks. My room was right across the hall from the emergency room so it was exciting when someone was being brought in. Most of the time it was as quiet as a church but when they got the call everyone rushed around doing whatever they had to do. I couldn't see into the emergency room from my bed so I would put this small mirror down by my right foot, the one that was free and using my toes I could position the mirror to see what was going on.

One night they brought in a guy they said was crazy. My nurse came in and closed all the curtains and told me to be quiet and they would have him out of there soon. I was scared and picked up the extra weight that was there for the traction. It was probably a couple pounds of cast iron. A little while later there was a lot of commotion and a man in a hospital gown came into my bed area with the intent of getting out my window. He shushed me, "Keep quiet, I just want to get out the window." He said. But to get out the window meant that he had to climb over me and the traction contraption. I was pretty sure that was not going to turn out well for me. People were in the hall so I held up the weight and threatened to hit him with it and yelled, "He's in here!" He looked a cross between pissed and frustrated as they came in and got him. He was gone a few minutes later and peace returned. Pretty exciting shit for a 12 year old with a broken leg.

I became very proficient at shooting rubber bands at a tissue target sitting by my left foot. I had to have the nurse retrieve the rubber bands from the floor for me when I ran out. They only did this for a short time and wouldn't come in to do it anymore. I learned I could hop as far out of the bed as I could and using my right foot's toes I would grab the rubber bands, hop back in bed and bring them in. I could pick up just about anything I dropped on the floor this way and I dropped a lot of things. Mom and Janet brought me crafts to work with and the camera and of course lots of books. I loved to read when I was a kid and had time to do it.

Being in traction meant I only had a sheet over my bottom half. One day two girls I barely knew came to visit me and they sat on the chair across the room. I asked them to come closer and they wouldn't which made me wonder why. I found out later that they sat there so they could see under the sheet and gaze upon my lovely 12 year old's package. After I realized what they were doing I would cover myself up when they came and they stopped coming soon after. Strange way to get your kicks isn't it. A guy would never do that to a girl would he... Yeah, I know.

I missed my dog Spike. He was just a regular dog pound dog, a mutt, no special breed or anything but he was mine and I missed him. I kept asking my Mom to bring him to visit but it was against the rules. One day everybody broke the rules and my Mom brought him in. My room was across from the E. R. which was just in from the back door and because I was so close they let Mom bring Spike to visit. He was sure glad to see me and tried his best to climb up on the bed. He only stayed a couple minutes but it was enough and I was happy. After all, what is a boy without his dog.

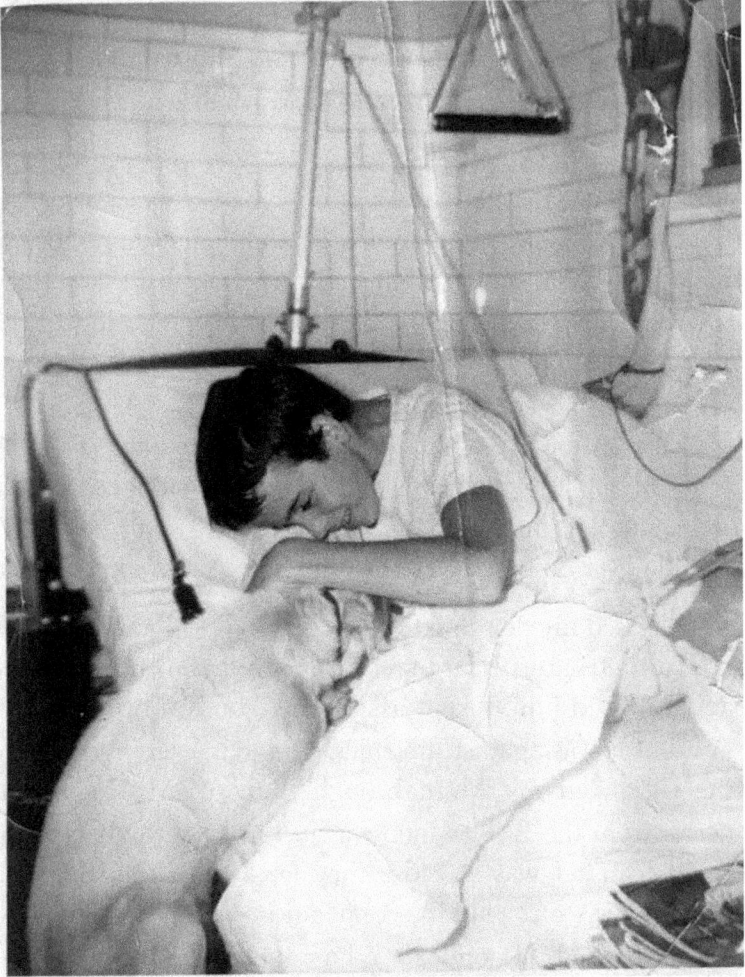

Finally came the day when the doc was going to remove the traction apparatus. He came in and unhooked the clamp from the rod through my knee and cut it off close to my skin on the other side and looked at my frightened and concerned face said, "This won't hurt" and pulled the rod out "a bit" He was right, I didn't feel a thing.

I was free. I could move around, go the bathroom like a normal human being but I had to keep weight off my left leg. My right one was very strong so this wasn't a problem. My left had atrophied from lack of use for 6 weeks and it would take time to build it back up again. They didn't have crutches for me yet so they gave me the light weight emergency room wheel chair and off I went. I explored every room in the hospital. I found the medical library and at night I looked in there for pictures or even drawings of female body parts to little avail. The nurses were always looking for me but I was able to evade them time and time again. That upper body strength gave me the power to make that wheel chair fly. There was one hall that ended in a tee with a water fountain. I could just get the wheel on the floor pedal to get a drink of water. I practiced coming flying down the hall, grabbing the left wheel and sliding into the water fountain. It took a few tries to perfect it and a dent or two on the water fountain but I finally got it.

I discovered the Solarium on the top floor corner of the hospital. It was different because it has asphalt tile rather than the terrazzo floors in the rest of the hospital. I was strong enough that I could grab the wheel down low and pull it up so fast that I "burned rubber." This left no mark on the terrazzo but left a nice 3 or 4 inch mark on the Solarium floor. So I did a lot of that and nobody knew it was me.

The next day while I was making my rounds after breakfast I rode down the hall to the Solarium to find the janitor on the floor trying to scrub the marks I left the day before. I froze in the doorway and he looked up and said,

"YOU!"

"STOP!"

"COME BACK HERE!

I only think he said the last two because as soon and he saw me I turned around and was flying down the hall to the elevator. I easily outran him but the jig was up. I didn't go back to my room for lunch and everyone in the hospital was on the lookout. They had more important things to do and nobody save for an Olympic runner could catch me anyway.

Finally hunger and darkness drove me back to my room. My nurse, the pretty one I had a crush on, was on duty and didn't have the full story or didn't care. She fixed me something to eat and I went to bed.

The next morning the head nurse was very sweet, everyone was very sweet. The head nurse was never sweet, she was a very stern, matter of fact woman. But that morning she was sweet.

"We have a new wheel chair for you to use today." She said ever so sweetly and took me to this ancient monstrosity made of wood with whicker seats. It was big, long and heavy and someone, probably the janitor from yesterday had tightened the bolts on the wheels so it took all my strength to move it. No more racing down the halls for me. Everyone smiled sweetly.

"How do you like it?" The head nurse said.

"Can't I have the other one? I asked stupidly.

"NO!" She said in no uncertain terms. So I made the best of it. I think the bearings were starting to loosen up by the end of the day but the janitor tightened them up for my next day's outing. I could barely make it from my room to the nurses station a few feet down the hall. Nobody ever scolded me because I had been bed bound for six weeks and was just letting off steam. But they weren't going to let me do it again either. Later that day I was fitted for crutches and sent home.

When I used the crutches I never let them come up to my armpits as you normally would. I was so strong that I could hold them against my side and just use my arms to hold me. In fact I could and did run with them that way. My stride was huge and I could cover a lot of ground. I was 12 and it didn't take long for my left leg to get strong enough to do away with the crutches and get back to my normal hellion ways.

Linda D and my First Kiss

Aww, ain't this going to be sweet. Awkward, embarrassing, well yes. Nice, absolutely. Sweet, well yes, sickeningly so.

Linda was my friend Curt's little sister. Curt was a year older than me and Linda was a year younger than me and really pretty.

One day I went to Curt's house to see if he wanted to go out and play. As I walked up the back stairs to their door I saw Linda through the curtains on the door and she was naked from the waist up. Her breasts were just starting to bud and I immediately fell in love. I stood quiet until she took the blouse she was ironing and went back to her room and then I knocked. We had hung out before from time to time but that was before I knew she had breasts. Before that she was just Curt's bratty little sister, breasts make all the difference, even though you could barely call them breasts yet.

"Is Curt here?" I asked.

"No, sorry, why?" she said.

"I wanted someone to play with." I said.

"Do you want to go out and play?" I said.

"Sure." She said and we left.

It was late afternoon and a warm sunny summer day. No school so we had all day to play. We went to Nay Aug park and watched people swimming, then down to the arcade and played some games. I showed her the monkeys at the zoo but we stayed in the back and giggled while we watched them fling poop at unsuspecting visitors. We watched Tilly the elephant in her cage swaying her head back and forth for a while. We talked about everything and nothing. I had come to appreciate a side of her that I hadn't known before, breasts or no breasts.

As it started to get dark we stopped and sat on a low wall in the alley that led to her house. We sat there talking about stuff. I told her about the swollen glands I had a few weeks ago and how I had to stay in bed.

"Where are these glands" she asked?

"Right here" I said and put my hand on my jaw.

"You can just feel them, they're about the size of a pea." I said.

She kept feeling her jaw to no avail. She couldn't find them.

"Here, I'll show you." I said

She was sitting on the wall to my right so I took my left hand and cupped her jaw and before either of us knew it I was kissing her. I didn't plan it, it just happened and she kissed me back.

All thought of swollen glands were forgotten as we sat there and kissed and kissed. Lights on porches came on and we moved down the alley to another wall that was indented behind a building and next to a tree and went back to kissing. No words were spoken, no need. We had both discovered something new that we both liked to do very much.

We were both too young to do anything more, we just kissed, a lot.

Kisses sweeter than wine, that was Linda D. My first kiss.

We then moved to Syracuse and I never saw her again. I tried looking up Curt when I visited years later but they must have moved by then and I couldn't find them.

Little things deflect us on life's path and I wonder occasionally what would have happened if we hadn't moved to Syracuse. Maybe I would have married Linda and had cute little blonde haired kids like her. That was not to be my fate and Syracuse was to become quite a shock for a 12 year old.

Moving to Syracuse

I was 12 when we moved. My Dad by then was working as a salesman on the road and his territory was New York Sate. Having to drive from Scranton to New York State was too far and Syracuse being in the center of the state was the perfect choice. The whole area is called Central New York to make that point. It is the crossroads of Route 81 and Route 690 that intersect in downtown Syracuse. The elevated train line that was parallel to the Eire Canal is now Route 690 and the Eire Canal as it goes through Syracuse is now Eire Blvd.

My father had scouted out some places for us to move to. We drove up on a weekend to look at them. The first was on the South side of Syracuse just as you came into town. It was over a garage that was behind a bigger house and my mother would have nothing to do with it. We looked at many more until she finally settled on the bottom half of a two family house on Herkimer Street. That's on the West side of town so you can see we covered the whole area.

The move up was uneventful for me. The biggest problem I had was leaving my old friends in Scranton and the different attitude of the girls in Syracuse. Girls in Scranton were very friendly while girls in Syracuse were aloof. In Scranton a girl would talk to me just like a boy would. In Syracuse it was like I smelled bad or something.

My mother enrolled me in Porter Jr High which was just a block away. I was nervous and scared because I didn't know anybody. At lunch some boys came up to me and asked that I go outside with them. Not suspecting a thing I went. In the school yard they informed me that to be accepted I would have to fight one of them. With no big brothers around to aid me I felt trapped. I had to fight one of them to be accepted at the school. I wasn't a fighter, I was a sensitive kid and I didn't want to fight. They told me I was going to fight one of them and I could pick one or they would pick one for me.

So I looked at the group and picked the smallest one.

He beat the crap out of me. We were sent to the principles office and my mother was informed of my introduction to school. She wasn't happy and neither was I. They put me on probation and considered me a troublemaker, a reputation I felt obliged to uphold.

VOCATIONAL, THE HIGH SCHOOL FOR TROUBLE MAKERS

The trouble makers at VO weren't the students, they were the teachers. In my experience back then most teachers were of one mold and if you didn't fit that mold you were cast off. As it turned out VO had the best teachers I ever had. That's because they were there to help you learn the best way each kid could learn. Unlike other teachers who just wanted every kid to be the same as every other kid. My grades at every school could be used as a measure of how good or bad the teacher was. Good inspiring teachers and I got good grades. I remember one English teacher told us we were going to read, "Johnny Appleseed" so I went home and read it.

The next day I discovered we were going to read the book in class at the speed of the slowest student. It took all semester to read one book. That teacher has to rank up there as the worst teacher I ever had and my grades reflected it. I would go to the school library every morning to get a new book that I would read by the next morning. I did much of my reading during the boring classes of which there were far too many.

One time in class when I was forced to read something I had already read I decided it was a good time for a nap. I put the book on the desk open in front of me and cupped my hands at my forehead blocking my closed eyes from the teacher's view. I was a light sleeper and I noticed the normal classroom buzz had stopped. Suddenly wide awake and unmoving I looked down to see the toes of my teachers brown leather shoes as he stood just behind me to my left. He caught me sleeping or so he thought. I pondered what to do for a moment and then took my right hand and turned the page of the book and resumed my previous posture. I got away with it yet again.

THE PRETTY BLONDE GIRL WHO RODE MY BIKE

We rode our bikes to her house, showing off, trying to catch her eye. I was too young to know exactly why but my genes were driving me just as they were for the rest of the boys. I guess the experience of boys acting stupid gave the girl an early lesson in how her womanly power held sway over her male counterpart. Everyone asked her to ride on their bike and for some unexplained reason she chose me. I was and am to this day flummoxed when confronted by beautiful women. It was hard for me not to do something stupid around them. But I gave her the ride and too embarrassed to stay, I sped home afterwards. I bet she didn't know why either. I sure didn't. I watched a nature show and there the male bird or whatever is doing weird things to attract the female and I think of the weird things human males do for the same goal. They make movies, write books and poems all about this sad state of affairs. I laughed at the movie with a, "Been there, done that" resignation in my head. I say to myself for the millionth time… If I only knew then what I know now…

My other girlfriend moved out of town. I had just started hanging out with her a few days before. Not the blonde, a different one. She was easy to be with which is the only reason I was with her. I went over the morning she was leaving to say goodbye even though it looked like rain. I watched her leave waving at me from the back window of her parents car while I sat on my bike in the street. It started to rain and I rode home getting a streak of mud up the back of my favorite striped shirt. I picked out the material with my Mom and she made the shirt for me. I remember shopping for the material and her wanting me to pick something different but the wild stripes of hues of blue and purple were what I wanted. The lights from the bar on the corner made the stripes on my shirt glow and I always liked walking by there at night so I could, "Light up."

I missed my new girlfriend but we never wrote like we said we would. We were young and both of us found other interests soon after she left.

Nice Horsey Down on the Farm

I was probably 14 or so when we were making our annual visit to the farm outside Oxford, PA. We would go down every summer for a couple weeks. Uncle Tim and Aunt Adelaid had five kids. My parents had five boys of which I was the youngest. They had four girls and one boy who was the youngest. Grace, the oldest was two months younger than me and we tended to hang out together.

The girls had a deal going where they boarded horses for a local riding stable that weren't quite ready for public use. The plan for the riding stable was that the girls would ride the horse and tame them. Everytime I went down they had a different horse. I was not a horseman. I never rode a horse and didn't really want too. The girls, especially Dot, who was and is a troublemaker, egged me on. Come on Frankie, you can ride it, it's easy, and so forth. Finally I agreed and they got the horse and an English saddle with the stirrups up too high. Grace looked on with her arms crossed across her chest and with a questioning frown on her face said to me, "Are you sure about this?" "Sure." I said. They said they couldn't adjust them any lower but I didn't believe them then and my mind hasn't changed.

I got up on the horse and they led me towards the alfalfa field. The horse seemed skittish or nervous and I wasn't very happy about the whole thing. "No problem," said Dot as she led the horse. One of them opened the gate and Dot let go of the reins as the horse and I passed through. Once clear of the gate the horse turned it's head and looked at me. A look I'll never forget. The next thing I saw was sky followed shortly after with a closeup view of alfalfa. As I rolled over looking for help there was no one in sight. I looked around and saw the backsides of the girls running down the hill after the horse who had a huge head start. So, left alone with my injuries, mostly a long scratch on my left arm from my wrist to my elbow, I got up and made my way back to the house. I had no interest in going after that horse, I didn't care if I ever saw it again and I sure wasn't going to try riding it again either.

Hours later the girls retuned with the horse. They apologized profusely but I didn't think Dot was very sincere what with that glint in her eye and all. Grace showed some concern for my scratch and I sat with my arm up so they all could see it. It wasn't deep but it was wide and stung like hell. I played it up for all it was worth. Dot kinda looked at me with that mischievous squint in her eye and I couldn't help but wonder what plans she was making for me. I'll have to keep a close eye on her from here on out.

Of Snowballs and Tough Kids

It was a cold snowy day and the three toughs from our school were trudging heads down, single file down the snow covered sidewalk in front of our house on Herkimer Street. Tom and I were in the attic making snowballs from the snow on the little roof just outside the window. First we hit the back of the head of the guy in the lead, he turned around and yelled at the guy behind him who protested innocence. Then we hit the second guy and he did the same to the last guy. Then we hit the last guy and the jig was up. But we were in the attic and there was nothing they could do. A bit later another kid we didn't like much walked by and we nailed a car just as it went by him. The driver stopped and gave the kid hell. The kid stood there arms outstretched claiming innocence, the driver said there was no one else around but him. All in all, a very satisfying day for snowballs.

THE GIRL THAT WANTED TO GO "ALL THE WAY"

She wanted to do it with one of us but we were too timid to follow through. We would sit on her porch swing, one on each side grabbing a feel now and then. We were like puppies wagging their tails and wanting to get petted but afraid to come close enough to get petted. All we did was wag our tails and bark. Finally Joe got the call and I was to go sit on the steps while he put his hand between her legs. And yes, afterwards he proudly let us smell his finger. But I was too timid and never got my chance. She gave up on us and likely found someone else to go "all the way" with. Just another example of the many missed opportunities in my life.

STRIPPERS AT THE FAIR

The New York State Fair is THE big deal for Syracuse. The huge fairgrounds are just outside the city limits but close to where I lived on Herkimer St. Of course we would go every year.

During the day Joe and I would walk through the main buildings looking at all the stuff and in the evenings we would pick up girls on the Midway.

We always succeeded at the first and we always failed at the second, but we never gave up, we just never succeeded.

This was a time when nudity was very rare. I found my Dad's cache of nudie magazines in the attic and that was a huge thrill. A huge step up from the pages of National Geographic's pictures of topless natives. I'm not sure why they always played volleyball though. I never saw a live naked boob and I was eager to correct that wrong.

Joe and I went to the fair looking to find something. There were several shows on the Midway that had girls, girls, lots of girls! They would entice the men in the audience to come in by parading the girls on a platform to the right and left of the barkers stand. There was going to be nude girls in there and we were too young to get in.

We wandered out back of the tent, hoping we could sneak in but the guards knew that before we did and chased us away.

We were hanging around one evening when a downpour came in and everybody ran for cover. The awnings of the food stands were full of people standing under them and we had no place to go so we climbed under what we thought was just a regular circus wagon. It had the all to familiar, "James Straights Shows" emblazoned on the side. The thing we didn't notice was that it butted up against the girlie tent. We sat there for a while waiting for the rain to stop when we heard a noise from above and looked up. There were cracks in the floorboards, small cracks and the floorboards were thick, probably 2 inches, but you could see a very narrow slice of what turned out to be the girls dressing room for the burlesque show. My first glance showed this woman with huge boobs putting her pasties on. I'll never forget that one of her nipples was slightly deformed. It had a little extra nipple colored flesh below the rest of it.

"There are naked women up there." I whispered to Joe

"We're under their dressing room!" I whispered.

He couldn't see any from where he was so he came over to where I was but by then she had her pasties on. Holy crap this was better than being in the tent. They would have pasties on in the tent but here they were naked as jaybirds. We kept moving back and forth trying to get a view of anything and I was hopeful of seeing everything. The rain was letting up and Joe and I constantly crashing into each other trying to see something might have made enough noise to attract the guard who came out and chased us away.

It was my first real live nipple sighting! Joe and I talked about that for days, often embellishing our story when we told it to the other guys to the point that they started to question whether we ever saw anything in the first place.

I like breasts very much. Maybe it was because I was breast fed and that made me want to do that again too. What guy doesn't want to do that. I often wonder which gender has it better. Women have all these things to entice a man, boobs, legs, etc. Men, well we only got the one thing and most of the time it ain't very impressive. On the other hand men are stronger and can get dressed and be ready to go in five minutes or less. Women need forever to get ready and when they finally are you can't touch them for fear of messing something up.

Generally I think it's better being a man. Just go to the restroom in a busy restaurant. Notice the line of women waiting to get in their bathroom, while you go straight in yours. I'm pretty sure I don't want to know what they do in there besides the obvious but it sure takes them a long time.

MODEL ROCKETS AND OTHER FOOLISHNESS.

My friend John and I didn't have much money and back then making a model rocket was expensive. John discovered that an old Hula Hoop was just the right diameter for the rocket motor. He took a piece of the hula hoop and painstakingly straightened it out. It looked pretty good. The first and last flight showed clearly that he did not get it straight enough as the rocket roared into the air in an arc that drove it into the ground a few seconds later.

My experiments went just as bad. I got this goofy idea to make a paint bomb. I can't quite remember why I wanted to do this. Perhaps the idea of it was all that mattered. I concluded that I could make a disposable rocket by gluing fins on the rocket motor itself and put a nosecone on top filled with yellow paint. My target was the intersection of Milton Ave and W. Genesee St. I carefully calculated the trajectory and set the launch pad just so and fired it off. I learned two things in the next microsecond. One is that the glue I used to attach the fins to the rocket motor was not adequate. Two, that without fins the rocket motor complete with the nosecone filled with yellow paint, would not fly in anything close to a straight line. My rocket motor got about 6 feet off the ground when the fins came off and from then on it was a desperate attempt to duck and run for cover as it ricocheted off the house, ground, garage and anything else foolish to stand in it's way. I never found the remains and I never tried that again.

BUILDING THE WILD MOUSE

The state fair comes to Syracuse towards the end of August and ends on the Labor Day weekend. About a week before the fair starts the James E. Straight shows comes in to put up the rides for the midway. You have to be old enough to have working papers to work at the fair and this was the first year I could do so. I walked out to the fair bright and early and went to the midway. The first and only ride to show up was the Wild Mouse, a roller coaster type of ride that was the biggest ride to be at the fair this year.

The Wild Mouse is still in use all over the world. The rides appeal beyond being a roller coaster were two factors. First on some curves at the top level the track extended beyond the frame of the ride several feet. Then the cars were long but the wheels were just under the center of it. As you rode the combination of the long nose and the track extending out beyond the framework gave you the impression it was going off the track and over the edge.

There was a large group of kids looking for jobs and the boss man did not pick me to work. The boss man was a tall foreboding no nonsense kind of guy. Looking back he reminds me of the head guard in Cool Hand Luke, the movie with Paul Newman. The boss man in the movie was the guy who always wore the mirrored sunglasses.

I decided to stay and watch, maybe one of the kids would quit and I could take his place. They started by laying out large planks in a big rectangle that would make up the foundation of the ride. The boss man used a transit and was very particular about getting it just right. Once they got that done they started unloading large, heavy 6X6 beams, each was painted white and had fittings attached to them in what seemed like random points. Although I couldn't see from my vantage point but they obviously had numbers on them to tell the boss man and his crew where each one went.

After doing this for an hour or so they had the first section assembled on the ground. One of the boss man's main crew got the crane and they jostled the big piece up. They tied it firm with ropes and started the whole process again on the next section. Once done with that they hoisted it up and attached cross braces from the first one to the second. This went on all day, the work hard and dirty. I could see some of the kids were really tired but none of them quit. Little by little hope dwindled for the small group of us who stayed to watch until there was just two of us. We talked and decided to come back the next day in case some of the kids did not show up.

The next day the two of us arrived early and sure enough some of the kids did not come back and we were hired. We started where they left off the day before. Hauling those large heavy 6X6 beams from the truck and assembling them to the ones on the ground. The fittings used were just plain old door hinges! Big ones on both sides of the joint but when it was pinned it made a very strong connection. One by one we assembled and erected the sections. At the end of the day I was more tired and dirty than I had ever been in my life. I had never worked so hard.

The boss man gave each of us a 'voucher,' a small white piece of paper with our name and how many hours we worked on it. He told us that we could exchange the 'voucher' for money when the pay wagon came later in the week. I was suspicious, having heard all the stories we all hear about carnival workers and complained that I wanted my money now. He said he didn't have it and I would have to wait like everyone else. I wasn't happy but there was nothing to do but trust him.

I came back the next day and we started in where we left off the day before. I was worried that I might lose my voucher so I put it in my shoe like I had seen people do on TV. One by one the sections went up until all of them were up. About three quarters of the way through the boss man noticed that things weren't going right and they got out the transit to check it. The whole assembly was out of whack and I thought we were going to have to take it back down to straighten it out. One of the boss man's crew, a huge guy, got out this large metal rod, about 8 feet long and went to the offending area. He put the rod under the foundation and with a great heave started moving the entire ride while the boss man looked through the transit. It was obvious they had done this before. In just a few minutes everything was OK and the huge guy put the rod away. Later on I got a close look at that rod, I could hardly lift it. That guy was stronger than any man I'd ever seen.

By the end of the third day we finished with the main foundation. The boss man said the hard work was over and the next day we would lay the track sections. I was relieved that we could start taking it easy as this was very hard work. I collected my voucher for the day and went to put it in my shoe with the one from the day before. I took off my shoe and all that was left of the first voucher was little bits of white paper rolled up like toothpicks. I took my handful of ground up voucher to the boss man and explained what happened. He said, "Tough kid, it's not my fault you did that" I went back to work, an entire days pay gone! At the end of the day the boss man gave me a new voucher and a smile. I guess these carney guys aren't as bad as the rumors suggest.

The next day I found out just how big a kidder the boss man really was. The track sections, each about 6 feet long were designed to be just a bit heavier that two 16 year old boys could easily carry. The first sections weren't bad because they went in on ground level. But the more track we laid the longer we had to carry them. After the level section we started on the first big climb that every roller coaster has. It was steep and got higher at every section. Two of the boss man's crew would bolt the new section we brought to the one before. There were two or three pairs of us kids bringing up the track sections and the boss man got the most work out of us by comparing our efforts to the other two crews. "Jesus you kids are slow, look at that other crew." He would say. The rail sections were made entirely of steel and they were covered with black grime that by the end of the day covered us completely. I was black from head to foot and more tired than ever but I was determined to see it through.

The last day was a bit easier as we brought up the last sections and did the small work of bringing the cars off the trucks to install on the track. The other rides started showing up and kids showed up to work on them. To my relief the pay wagon showed up and we all got paid in real money. The boss man thanked me for the good work and said that his regular crew could finish it up the next day. He offered to let us ride free when the fair started. I came by a few days after the fair started but the guy who was running the ride, who I had worked beside for three days pretended he didn't know me and wouldn't give me a free ride. I paid for a ride but I didn't enjoy it very much. Several days later a part of one of the cars came off and jammed into the track hurting a kid and his father. They shut down the ride for the rest of the fair and I didn't go back to help take it down. Not getting that free ride really soured it for me. I felt sorry for the people that got hurt and I was glad they had to shut it down and glad the fault was with nothing I was involved in. Still I treasure those three days, the hard work, the experience, even the dirt.

MY MOTHERS TOOTHPASTE TEST

For those who don't remember Brylcreem. It is a white hair grease and came in a red and white tube very similar to the Colgate toothpaste we used then.

One evening we were all in the darkened TV room watching TV. My mother came into the room from the bathroom holding up her toothbrush in her hand and just stood there, backlit from the bathroom light. After several moments we all stopped watching TV and looked at her wondering why she was just standing there. Once she had our full attention she announced. "I've just done a test and I have found that Brylcreem does not make a very good toothpaste." Whereupon she turned around and went back into the bathroom.

FRANK THE PHOTOGRAPHER

My Dad got into the hobby of photography when I was very young or perhaps just born. Because of that we have many hundreds of pictures of my childhood until I was about 5. We have some 8MM movies too, in color, from my early teen years. I even have the old 8MM movie camera he used. When I became interested in photography I used his old 35MM camera and took what pictures I could afford to buy film for. I even made a darkroom in the basement of our house on Herkimer Street in Syracuse.

I didn't have an enlarger so I went to the store to look at them. They looked really nice but I didn't have near enough money to buy one. But my Dad's old 35MM camera had a feature I thought I could use. The back of the camera slid down and off to allow putting the film in. I made a frame out of balsa wood to hold the camera up against the light box that was used for contact prints.

A regular enlarger works from overhead and shines light down to a table below. You move the head up and down to get the size you want. I couldn't do that so I made mine horizontal. I then made a frame out of balsa and stuck that to the darkroom wall. This would hold the photo paper and block out the edges to give it the white edge you see on a professional print.

I developed the film leaving the header and tail piece on so I could install it back in the film canister and put it in my makeshift enlarger. I dried the film by pushing it into a cardboard tube that was just a bit narrower than the width of the film and used a hair dryer connected to the tube to dry it quickly.

I then loaded the negatives back into the film canister and put it in the camera like you would ordinary 35MM film. Setting the light box on it's side I moved it back in forth until I got the enlargement I wanted and used the focus on the camera with the little screw stop removed.

Once it was all set I turned off the lights and with the red safe light on I would load the paper into my wall holder and turn on the light box for the few seconds it took to expose the film.

From there on out it was standard developing procedure. I reasoned that because I was using the same camera as an enlarger that I took the pictures with, any anomalies in the lens would be offset.

For a test one day I took a grain of salt and put it on a piece of scotch tape and put that on the camera-enlarger where the film went. I made a 4x5 picture of that grain of salt. But I had to wait till dark because I had to move the light-box across the cellar to get it that big and it took a long time to expose it. You would be amazed at how good that worked and how sharp the picture was.

I have many boxes of photos, like all families, and I know I have a few of the ones I took and developed and printed. It brings back good memories of a fun time. By the way, the above procedure took a lot of time and an enlarger would have saved much of that. But then what story could I tell now. Many of the pictures in this book are those my father took and developed on his own.

That Last One Half Inch Did It

Being the youngest of five boys had some perks and some not so perks. Go ahead, you try to find the word that is the opposite of perk. Some say it is a krep, but nobody knows what a krep is and don't tell me it's the opposite of perk.

Back to my story. Jeez I barely get started and I run into this. So again, back to my story. Boy things were much easier before I gave up coffee. I hope I remember to delete this foolishness.

Being the youngest of five boys had some good things and bad things. There that's better. The good things were I rarely got beat up at the playground as the other boys all thought I would call one of my bigger brothers to beat them up. It was good that they thought this because it might not have been true. I never had to test it though. The other perk I got was lots of slightly worn clothes to wear, fully tested by my brothers before me, how swell. Some of it even fit … sort of. My mother was good at tailoring and managed to make it all fit eventually. Shoes were different and I remember one day going to the shoe store and putting my foot in the X-ray machine to see how well the shoe fit. They banned those once they found out they caused cancer. If I get cancer in my right foot I can blame that shopping day.

Being the youngest I was also the smallest and as the last born I was, "The baby" in the family. I used to say, and still do, that my parents kept trying and trying to have the perfect child and stopped once they did.

In other words I didn't get any respect.

Until that magical day when I discovered that I was taller than everybody else. It was only one half inch but it made all the difference in the world. It was hard for my brothers to give me any crap when to do so they had to look up to me. I was skinny as a rail and a strong wind would have blown me over but I was taller and that's all that mattered. I wasn't tall. I watched the measurements on the wall, 5' 10" - 5' 11" - 5' 11 ½" and that's where it stopped. At 15 I so wanted to be six foot tall but I never made it. Today I'm going the other way and am down to 5' 10" but I tell the nurse when she weighs me in that I'm 5' 11" because if I told her my real height there charts and graphs would say I was obese. Not so at 5' 11." It's an old joke to say I'm not overweight, I'm under height. However I justify the lie because there was a time when I was 5' 11" and the fact I lost an inch is due to my back compressing, so in the interest of scientific accuracy I say 5' 11."

My height was and is normal, neither tall nor short, height was never an issue to me. At some point I began to notice how it affected other people. Tall men tended to get more respect and short men get less. Many women won't date a short man instead they look for the perfect man, the "Tall, dark and handsome" one. So the almost 6 foot height never affected me with the opposite sex. I didn't need that to screw up, I could do that all on my own.

Most of the time, hell, all the time I didn't know what girls wanted or why. I kinda thought they were this pretty pure thing that smelled good and I could never understand why they would ever want to have anything to do with us boys. When one did, I didn't know what to do.

With age and experience I've come to understand that I will never understand women but now I've learned to stop trying. It's kinda like when you were a kid and someone hands you an ice cream cone. Don't ask why and wait for the ice cream to melt, just eat the damn thing and say, "Thank you, may I have more?"

THE SUMMER OF THE GREEN PLAID CAP

When I was a kid my mother always cut my hair, that is until one day when she received, as a gift, an electric hair cutting kit. It had all the attachments from a buzz cut to a flattop. What she lacked for in experience the razor made up for in efficiency. I sat there in the kitchen with the towel around my shoulders to catch the hair and she approached with the new toy. Buzzes went the razor, "Boy this sure cuts fast" went my mother. "What happened" went I. On the floor went my hair. After only a few moments I decided that something was very wrong. I was feeling coolness on areas of my scalp that never felt cool before. She insisted that she could fix it but I refused.

I put on a green plaid baseball hat and walked to the barber shop. The barber looked sadly at my head said the only thing he could do was to cut it all off. All of this explains why I wore a green plaid cap all that summer and why that was the last time I let my mother cut my hair.

What goes around comes around. Now at 66 and not having enough hair to make paying a barber worthwhile. I have taken to using a home haircutting kit just like my Mom used way back then. My first attempt took a long time as I tried several different gauges to see what length worked for me. After doing it several times I have settled on the ¼ inch one. I just use that all over every couple of weeks and in five minutes I'm done. I used to do it in the bathroom but hair got everywhere so not I do it outside and use the leaf blower to clean up afterwards. Both the carport and me. There's nothing subtle about me I'll tell you.

Chooch the Cat

Chooch was my cat. I got her when I was 16 and she died when I was 32 at the age of 16. Odd how those numbers worked out. That hair lick on her back was a distinctive feature that you could never get to stay down. She seemed to know when her picture was being taken and always posed for it. She was a girl after all.

A friend asked me if I would take his mother cat and five kittens. I said sure ... without asking my mother about it ... not a very good idea. I built a small chicken wire fenced in area next to the garage for them but my mother insisted I get rid of them. After a few days we reached an agreement where I could keep one of the kittens. Of the five kittens, two were identical twins with one exception. One always cried when you picked it up, the other didn't. Wisely, I decided I wanted the one that didn't. The people came to get the mother cat and kittens and I went out and picked up one of the twins, it cried and I put it in the box with the others. After they were long gone I went to get my new kitten and bring her into the house. I picked her up, she cried, shit, I gave away the wrong cat!

I named her Chooch and she came to live in my room. As she grew up I wanted her to have easy access to the outside so I built a ramp outside my window that she could climb up and get in or out as she wished. I was a liberated kind of guy back then and a Beatnik so that's the way I was.

One day while I was sleeping Chooch stuck her head through the curtains from outside and made a muffled meow, kinda a, "Merfh" kind of sound because she had a baby field mouse in her mouth. I looked up and she dropped the mouse and disappeared back out through the curtain. Meanwhile the mouse ran under the bed.

I leaned out of the bed far enough to look under to see about 5 more mice huddled in the corner fearing for there lives. "Oh crap!" I said and got out of bed and tried to catch the mice. "Merfh" and Chooch arrived with another live mouse. "Stop that!" I said and continued trying to catch one of the little bastards. I caught one and threw it out the window only to have Chooch bring it back in. She was not pleased that I was returning her gift and kept trying to bring them back in. Finally, I put Chooch out of my room and collected the mice and put them out the window. I didn't let Chooch out for a couple days to give the mice time to escape. Not that I gave a rats ass for the mice, I just didn't want them living under my bed.

Later that summer Chooch did it again but this time with a robin sized bird. I didn't hear the "Merfh" this time. Instead I was awakened by the bird flying around the room with Chooch in hot pursuit. Floor to dresser to bed to floor was what I awoke too. "What the hell is going on?" I said as

I huddled under the covers what with the flapping wings of the bird and that damn cat racing around the room. It took me by complete surprise as it's nothing you'd ever expect to wake up too. I peeked out from under the covers and made several attempts to catch the cat. Chooch was single minded and the bird was firmly in her sights. With claws flying she escaped me time and time again. If only that damn bird would alight somewhere maybe I could catch the cat.

Finally with feathers flying around the room I captured the cat and managed to shove her out of the door. Then I opened the window and after far too many attempts I managed to get that idiot bird out of the window. While all of this is going on my father is outside the door.

"What the hell is going on in there? He said.

"Don't open the door, there's a bird flying around in here." I said.

"Why in Christ's name do you have a bird in there?" He said.

"Chooch brought it in, I'm trying to get it to go out the window." I said.

"Just get rid of the damn bird, I'm trying to sleep." He said.

Well, hell, what did he think I was trying to do!

My parents bought a house on Lincoln Park Drive and we moved from Herkimer Street there with Chooch. My bedroom was too high from the ground for a ramp for her and the windows were the awning type which further complicated it. But I was a Beatnik by then and spending a lot of time on the hill which was only about a mile away across Eire Blvd, a four lane road built where the Eire Canal used to go through Syracuse.

Chooch would follow me around like an aloof dog. By that I mean she was always nearby but not at my side. She was like a ghost. I would leave a friends apartment and by the time I'd walked a hundred feet or so there was Chooch following along. She rarely went inside with me preferring to stay out and lurk. She became a fixture. "Look here comes Frank and Chooch" was the common refrain.

I was so used to her just being around that I tended to forget about her. The only time this was a problem was when it came time to cross Eire Blvd. Chooch was a very cautious cat and she would only cross a street if there were no cars in sight. I crossed Eire Blvd on a straight section and even when traffic was low there was still a car Chooch could see. I would forget this almost every time until I'd gotten a block or so and noticed she wasn't there. I'd look back and there was Chooch sitting on the curb, leaning way out and watching right and left for cars and not moving. "Crap!" I said and walked back to get her. Even when I held her in my arms to cross the street she would strain back and forth to look for cars.

Other than that she was an okay cat to have around.

The Power Of The Mighty Boob!

I've speculated about the power of the boob most of my life. What is it about them that makes men and boys go absolutely nuts. A lot of it may be because we don't have them or it might trigger something in our genes that says, "Look! Food!" That would explain why men tend to like bigger boobs over smaller ones. But trying to see them is something every red blooded American male strives to do and we'll act damn stupid in the process.

The late 50's brought in the braless era. Where women suddenly realized that by letting those puppies go free under their blouses would drive men crazy. I think that and hot pants were the highlight of my life. But I digress. The subject is boobs. When girls went braless, the jiggling began. Oh, what sweet memories or should I say mammaries.

Bada boom!

One day I was driving down S. Crouse Avenue approaching Marshall Street in my Dad's car behind a delivery truck. Just as I passed Marshall Street a girl in a thin white blouse with large braless boobs came out of a shop door and turned up S. Crouse. She had dark nipples easily showing through the thin blouse and she jiggled her way up S. Crouse.

Out of the corner of my eye I saw the break lights on the truck in front of me and slammed on my brakes. A moment later I heard the squealing tires of the car behind me and a moment after that the squealing tires of the car behind him. I watched the girl disappear around the corner to Marshall Street and looked in my rearview mirror to see the guy behind me doing the same thing. That gal almost caused a three car and one truck pileup and I'd bet she never knew it. But then again maybe she did. In any case it's got to be a big ego boost to know what power those jugs have over men.

After braless came the halter top. These little beauties were worn braless and involved a very deep V neck down to the belly button and were bare in the back. The two small pieces of cloth were tied loosely around the back of the neck. You got to see just about everything except the nipple in one of those and were my favorite piece of woman's attire of the time.

Hot Pants came along about that time as designers were eager to see how little they could get women to wear. You can't get any shorter than Hot Pants as they got to the top. They followed short shorts which I liked more. At least they left something to the imagination. My favorite short shorts were white and worn by the Dallas Cowgirls. What made them very hot was the tiny inch long slit up the side. I can't explain why, it just is.

Mini Skirts became popular then too and this probably increased sales for matching panties because it's damn near impossible for a girl to not show them wearing a true miniskirt. Despite that my favorite was the Dallas Cowgirls hot white short shorts with the slit.

I guess I'm a slit man and I make no excuses for it.

The Last Fight

Tom was two years older than me to the day, our birthday is on the same day, March 25. I guess those hot summer nights were very fertile times for my parents.

When we were very young I would always get a cookie for Tom when my Mom gave me a cookie. As we grew older things changed. The teenage years were especially bitter for both of us. We fought often. One day for reasons I've long forgotten and when nobody was home we got into a bitter brawl. I was so pissed at him that I grabbed the rabbit ears from the TV.

I grabbed this by the base, the ball, and whipped Tom with it. That ended that fight and he went into his room. He never fought with me again. I'd be willing to bet he had some welts from it but he wouldn't admit it ever, even today I'd bet. Of course by that time I was as big as he was and boy did that make a difference.

For my part I had to spend the rest of the afternoon trying to bend the antenna back straight. A chore I can tell you. They worked just fine but they had that kinda Fred Flintstone look to them. That evening as we watched TV my father stared at them for a bit and said, "What the hell's wrong with those rabbit ears?" We just shrugged and he gave up on it. After five boys I guess he just accepted crap like that.

Tom and I got along much better after that but there was something that always pissed me off…

IT WAS NEVER TOM'S FAULT

My father had this annoying tendency to always take Tom's side whenever something went wrong and I never knew why. That changed when we got old enough to drive. For example, one day Tom took my English bike without asking me and gave a friend a ride on the handlebars. He hit a curb and destroyed the front tire. It cost me $12 to fix it and my father would not make Tom pay for it. Tom's attitude was that it wasn't his bike so why should he have to pay to fix it. It took me decades for the right moment to get even and boy did it please me to do it.

Tom was married and had one son, Chuck, who was racing BMX. By then I was living on the lake and had our Mom living with me. Tom would brag about Chuck ad nauseam to all of us to the point where we dreaded seeing him. Occasionally one of Chuck's races would bring Tom and his family close enough to visit Mom. One year he bragged about how much this special bike of Chuck's cost, about two grand as I recall and I just noted that and stored it in the back of my mind. He also said this very expensive bike was very light weight and would only hold someone the weight of Chuck who probably weighed 60 pounds or so at the time.

Okay, that sets the stage.

A year or so later Tom was visiting after a race and I said to him.

"Let's take a look at this bike Chuck races." I said. The conversation about it being frail long forgotten I'm sure.

Tom took the bike out of the back of his van and set it on the ground. I held the handle bars and pretended to be interested in the features and why it made it so expensive. Tom was standing a few feet away when I got my revenge…

I swung my leg over the cross bar and sat down in the seat, well, not really, I had my weight on my left leg and it just looked to Tom as if I was sitting on the seat.

"Let's take this puppy for a ride and see what's so hot about it." I said as I leaned forward and made like I was about to do just that.

Tom almost shit his pants. "NO, NO, It'll break! It isn't strong enough to hold you." He yelled.

I weighed somewhat over 200 at the time and I was damn sure that was what would happen if I really was to ride it. But I wasn't through.

"Hell, for two grand it ought to hold me." I said and I again made like I was going to ride it.

Tom was beside himself, "Jesus, you'll break it, please get off." He said.

So I reluctantly got off but not until I had exacted maximum revenge, but before Tom passed out.

"Christ, not much of a bike if you can't ride it. I think you got screwed Tom." I said and turned around and walked away with that smug smile of satisfaction on my face as Tom stayed back and examined his precious bike for any damage.

And retelling the story feels just as good today as doing it did then. I never told Tom I did this, so Tom, if you're reading this… Gotcha! We're even now. Best $12.00 I ever spent.

Phyllis, the Gal who Took My Virginity

Well, actually I gladly gave it up. Hell, when I was a kid another kid told me it was lined with a sandpaper like substance and would grind you up if you ever put your dick in there. That haunted me for years.

~~~

George had a bum leg. His left leg was at least 3 inches shorter than his right and he wore one shoe with a big lift so he could walk. He still had a bad limp but because he was tall the other kids didn't bother him. His girlfriend was Phillis who he referred to as a nymphomaniac. He told me of one evening while he was sitting in her living room with Phyllis and her single Mom. They were passing notes back and forth. She said in one that he, "Couldn't touch her with a ten foot pole" He replied that, "She couldn't take a ten foot pole if he had one" I was a virgin and I was just fascinated by what he was telling me.

Some months after they broke up Phyllis took on the task of helping me lose my virginity. But I didn't know it at the time. I was just trying to be nice to her and losing my virginity didn't seem likely for me. I was over at their second floor apartment when Phyllis asked me to go out in the back yard to play. We went out and sat on the steps. She started by snuggling up to me and sticking her tongue in my ear which really started the juices flowing.

Then she got up and started goofing around and tagging me trying to get me to tag her. This went on for a while. She had a funny look in her eye that I didn't recognize at the time. (She was horny) Finally she grabbed my hand and pulled me into the basement where she proceeded to strip and dragged me to the back.

It was not romantic at all and not sexy. But I did my best to keep up. I was new to screwing and I didn't understand the angles involved with screwing a shorter girl while standing up. I tried to pick her up but that didn't work. I tied squatting down and that didn't work. It didn't help having her urging me on with that sense of urgency. I have never been in charge of my dick, it's gets hard when it's damn ready too, even if I don't want it to. A mind of it's own that little bastard has, that's for sure.

My first attempt at getting laid turned out to be a huge failure and we gave up. We came out of the cellar with me in front and Phyllis behind buttoning her blouse. There was her Mom who said, "The cellar, really, the cellar, get upstairs" she said to Phyllis and "You go home" she said to me.

You would think that this rebuke would be the end of it and for me it would have ended there. But Phyllis was determined to get my virginity and when she heard my parents were out of town she showed up on my front porch with a bag. She had run away from home and wanted to stay with me for, "Just a day or two" My brother Tom wasn't out of town although he wasn't home right then. So I let her in and took her down to my basement.

We took out a big old chase lounge, one of two my parents had. It was the size of a single bed. I got some sheets and bedding from upstairs for her. That night she made a man of me. It was awkward, uncomfortable and glorious as I fumbled in the dark trying to figure out the lay of the land, so to speak, of a woman's body. She did some things and soon we did it. I was no longer a virgin... Finally! I thought I had discovered a cure for cancer and I wanted to tell the world about it. Instead I did more research...

The next morning I could hear Tom upstairs getting breakfast and then his car driving out of the driveway. We moved operations to my bedroom. Now I could see what I was doing and where I was going. Phyllis was a beautiful girl and we did it a lot.

Phyllis was wearing both me and her welcome out. She had a reputation as a nymphomaniac and I wouldn't dispute that. I was ready for her to leave but I didn't know how to get her to go. My friend Leo showed up one evening and we shot the breeze for awhile. My parents were still out of town and Tom wasn't around. Leo suggested we should all get in his Dad's car and drive to New York City. We knew some people there but we weren't quite sure where they were, somewhere in the village and we thought we could find them once we got there.

At about 1AM the three of us piled in the car. Leo driving, me in the passenger seat and Phyllis curled up in the back seat and was soon asleep. Phyllis was very open about what we had been doing and Leo was very curious about it too. He was still a virgin and wanted to know everything I could tell him. I suspected Phyllis wasn't sound asleep and could probably hear us so I kept it low and not the detail I would have given out had she not been in earshot. The hours passed and the sky started to lighten which woke Phyllis up. She climbed over the bench seat to sit between us. Soon she turned her attention to me. She started to kiss my neck and fool around with my ear in an effort to get me interested in joining her in the back seat. But I was embarrassed with Leo there and wasn't rising to the occasion which Phillis discovered when she put her hand on my crouch.

Without batting an eye she turned to Leo and started to do the same thing to him. After hearing all the things that went on between Phyllis and me over the last few days Leo was indeed rising to the occasion. He asked me if I minded and I said no. I was glad she had turned her attention to him. I was spent. He pulled the car over and the two of them retired to the back seat and I started driving. The sun had just come up and soon I could see Leo's bleached white ass bobbing up and down, like a lighthouse beacon.

I watched the rear view mirror, trying to avoid seeing Leo's ass, for traffic heading our way. A tractor trailer approached and as he started to get close I slowed down to reduce the window of opportunity to see the two of them going at it in the back seat. My maneuver worked and he passed by unaware or uncaring about what was going on. Traffic was light and I was hoping Leo would finish before another vehicle came by.

I saw a car in the passing lane catching up to us going pretty fast. I waited till he was just behind us when I let off on the gas and he scooted by. But then just as he passed I saw his brake lights come on and the passengers in both the front and back seats with their faces to the window. As he slowed I sped up. Then he sped up and I slowed. Meanwhile Leo's ass kept bobbing, mooning the world as it were. The other car and I danced out little dance with their passengers laughing and pointing until a loud ARGH! came from the back seat. Leo's ass stopped bobbing and the other car sped off.

After a time I pulled over and the two of them got in the front seat as we were before. Leo had a shit eating grin on his face and I congratulated him of losing his virginity. Phyllis was quiet for a bit and then announced she had to go to the bathroom. The next rest area was too far and she demanded we get off at the next exit. It was a little town whose name escapes me now. We were about 4 hours out of Syracuse on the NYS Thruway so I guess we were somewhere near New Paltz. It was a very small town and not much was open. Leo pulled into a small diner but Phyllis said it wouldn't do and we should look for someplace else. She was being a bitch about it for reasons only she knew and I was cementing my conclusion that she was nuts. We pulled into another diner and that wasn't good enough either. These early morning actions drew the attention of a local cop just starting his shift and he pulled us over.

Leo rolled down his window and the cop asked, "What brings you to our fine city so early in the morning?" "We're on our way to New York City and the lady had to use the restroom so we got off the Thruway to look for one." Leo said. "What was wrong with the two you stopped at?" "The lady didn't like them." Leo said. At that point the cop leaned down and asked Phyllis how old she was. "16." she said. Leo said he was 17 and I said 16 too. Then the cop asked Phyllis what she was doing with the two of us.

"I was having sex with them which is why I need to go to the bathroom." She said matter of factually. The bitch!

"Everybody out of the car NOW!"

The cop said and he put Phyllis in the back seat of his cruiser. "You two follow me to the station and don't try anything funny. You're in big trouble!" He said.

Why the hell did she say that we wondered and I opined that I was now absolutely sure Phyllis was nuts.

We pulled in next to the cop and two other officers escorted us into the station while the first cop took Phyllis somewhere in the back. We were allowed to just sit and ferment. The cop at the small desk across the room told us to keep quiet which made it all worse. After about two hours the first cop came and got us and took us back. Phyllis was nowhere in sight. He told us we could be charged with statuary rape and we were lucky we got caught before we crossed the state line into NJ. That would be transporting a minor across state lines. He tried to be stern and forceful but I began to suspect that after spending two hours with Phyllis that like me, he might have concluded that she was nuts also. He then let the bomb drop. He was going to let use go. We were momentarily elated. Then he told us they had called Phyllis's mom and Leo's dad and they were driving down together to get them. He told me he couldn't reach my parents but did get ahold of my brother Tom who was coming down to get me.

We were sent back out to the front room to wait. Leo was dejected and didn't know how he was going to deal with his dad. I thought it was her mother he should worry about. His dad would drive him back in their car and Phyllis would go back with her mother in her mothers car. He just had to spend four hours in the car with his dad, who was a SU football player in his youth. I didn't envy him. I just hoped Tom would get here before they did.

The hours dragged and finally Tom showed up. I wanted to leave right away because I figured Leo's dad couldn't be far behind. I needn't have worried as it took the two of them an hour to get going where Tom left right away. After getting another lecture while I paced in place from one foot to the other. The cop finally looked at me long and hard and said. "You want to get out of here before her mother shows up don't you." "YES." I said and he smiled. He had been dragging it out on purpose just to see me squirm. Sadistic bastard! "Okay, get out of here." He said and I damn near dragged Tom out the door. He wasn't too eager to face Phyllis's mom either because we left in a hurry.

Several days later on a hot summer night, I was watching TV wearing just a pair of light blue Bermuda shorts, no shirt, no shoes, not even socks, just the shorts when the doorbell rang. I opened the door to find Phyllis standing there looking all sweet and innocent.

"I left my stuff in your bedroom, can I come in and get it." She said.

"Sure, no problem." I said and let her in while I stood at the door with her mother who had been standing behind her glaring at me. I felt naked and didn't know what to say so I just stood there hoping it would all end soon.

Looking at me sternly she said, "And I thought you were a nice boy."

"I was until I met your daughter" I said...

Silently...

To myself.

Phyllis came back clutching her stuff and being ever so sweet. She was enjoying my embarrassment a little too much. I was never so glad to see someone leave. I watched them go down the porch steps thanking my lucky stars my parents weren't home. That was the end of my relationship with her but as you can tell, I never forgot her.

I envy todays kids with the information available to them. Back in 1961 I didn't have a clue and didn't know where to get one. None of my friends did either. We were all sloshing around in that warm wet swamp trying to figure it out as we went.

John's Scooter

John driving, Frank, Tom and Bruce sitting on the spare tire. The Herkimer Street house is in the background.

The middle brother, John, was the oldest brother living at home in my teenage years. Mom was working at University Hospital so John could get a break on tuition at Syracuse University where he was studying to be an Electrical Engineer. He had a part time job at Syracuse China as well and needed transportation. He bought a Lambretta Motor Scooter. With five raging horses under the seat it had power a plenty for city driving. I was 15 and not old enough to get a drivers license to drive it legally but I was old enough to sneak out late at night, steal it by pushing it out the driveway for about a block and then start it up and ride for hours going no where for no reason. In the middle of a Syracuse winter no less. Proof, if you needed it, that 15 year old teenagers are stupid beyond belief.

There were problems with this. For one it didn't start well in the cold. But not a big problem as we lived on a hill. I would take it out of the garage and push it a half block to the top of a small hill, hop on, let out the clutch and it would start … except that one time when it didn't. I had to push it to the top of the next hill about ⅓ mile away. This hill was smaller and when it didn't start then I was screwed because I was at the bottom of all the hills. I was on W. Genesee Street in front of the CoCo Cola plant.

With no other choice I pushed it as fast as I could, jump on and let out the clutch and it didn't start. I did this for hours. Desperate because it would be light soon and my family would get up and John would see his scooter and I were missing. Back and forth I went until a cop walking home from work saved me. He put his briefcase down, said, "Get on, I'll push you" and we got it started. I was both nervous and trying to think of what to say so I offered to give him a ride. He laughed, "No thanks" he said and I went straight home.

I stopped about a half block away from home and pushed the scooter into the garage and went to bed. I got maybe an hours sleep before I had to get up for school. But it was worth it, I was on the road and driving. Nobody I knew saw me so I got no credit for it but I was driving and they weren't.

MOTORIZED HIJINKS. (JUMPING THE SCOOTER)

Here is Ozzy pretending to balance the scooter, which was on the kickstand and not moving at the time.

My friend Ozzy came over to hang out one day. They had just paved Herkimer Street in front of the house and we checked it out. They made curbs by forming asphalt around the storm drain out in front to control the water. In so doing it also formed a ramp which gave us the idea. I started by taking John's scooter and coming in from the street and jumping it over the curb onto the front lawn. We took turns each getting closer to the drain where the ramp got steeper and steeper. Man was this fun!

The scooter had a kick stand. The type where you step on it and pull the scooter back. It was a casting, probably aluminum, that was under the floorboards with just a little paw that you pushed down with your foot. The part that stopped it in the upright position also hung down forming something very similar to a hook. This becomes important to know because as we moved to the steeper part of the curb that hook got closer to the soft asphalt. We didn't realize it at the time. It was Ozzy who dared to make the big jump as near to the storm drain as possible and when the kickstand hook met the top of the asphalt curb, the scooter stopped as if in mid flight. The front wheel high off the ground and impaled at a 45 degree angle. But although the scooter stopped, Ozzy didn't. He did a front flip over the handle bars landing on his butt on the grass with nary a scratch on him. It took us some time to get the scooter unstuck and to my surprise it didn't hurt it one bit.

By now you know the scooter was mine. John had moved on to a car, a 1956 Chevy, blue and white. One of those two tone jobs. It was really nice. It really belonged to his fiancee Peach and he had repainted it in our backyard. One day he had to go to Syracuse University to pick up something and I tagged along. We found a parking place, the last parking place next to the driveway that led into the building he was going too. After we got what he came for we headed back to the car to find a VW bug parked so close to the front of John's car that he couldn't get out. It was so close because it would have blocked the driveway otherwise.

"What do we do now?" I asked.

He didn't say a thing and didn't seem perturbed either. I guessed we were just going to sit in the car and wait for the VW bug owner to come out and move. John, without saying a word, started the car, put it in drive and slowly inched forward until we were in contact with the VW's bug rear bumper. Then he gave it just enough gas to push the VW bug forward so that it completely blocked the driveway, which was further than he needed to go to get out. Then he just backed up and pulled out of the parking place leaving the VW bug to fend for itself. I would have liked to sit on the grass across the street to see what happened. That was a busy driveway which led into the building so I think the VW bug's owner must have gotten in trouble but I'll never know. You gotta watch John, he is one of those strong silent types that rarely, as in never, loses his temper. Except for that one time he got so mad at me out at camp and gave me a swift kick in the butt that hurt for hours. But other than that he was always pretty cool.

Mr. Fuck at Newfoundland

You're not going to believe this and I was tempted to leave it out. But it's true so here it is.

When I was 16 I had my driver's licensee. So it was no chore for me to drive from the camp to Newfoundland every day to get the newspaper. My father had one 'reserved' at the local drugstore. Pop's paper was one of many that people reserved. This was done by writing the name in pencil in the upper right hand corner of the front page. The papers were stored to the right just as you went into the store on a metal radiator cover by the window. The cover was just the right width and was about the height of a coffee table. The papers were placed so that all the names were visible and it was easy to pick yours out. Every morning I went through this ritual of entering the store, riffling through the pile looking for, "Hogg" written in pencil and then walking the 10 feet or so to the old fashioned soda fountain.

The pharmacist, who worked at the rear of the store in an elevated area dispensing drugs would sometime call out a greeting. Like most small towns they were very friendly. I would climb up on the old swivel stool. You might remember the type with red plastic covers and chrome rings alternating with red around the sides. The countertop was marble and the back bar had all the neatly organized containers for syrup and other ingredients. There was a place for the ice cream scoops to set in water and a place to mix up milk shakes. I would order a shake or an ice cream soda or sometimes a banana split. My favorite ice cream soda was chocolate with chocolate ice cream. I would read the paper while enjoying my treat.

One day after entering the store I turned right as always and scanned the papers for 'Hogg" written in pencil in the upper right corner when I noticed the name "Fuck"! I stopped dead in my tracks. Nah couldn't be, must be "Tuck" or something like that. I considered asking the lady behind the soda fountain then thought better of it. After all, I was only 16.

Every day after that I looked for the "fuck" paper. Some days it was there, some days not. I guess on those days he had gotten there before me. But sure enough it was "fuck." There was no mistaking it. I figured that they must not know what that word means way out here in Newfoundland. Perhaps it was pronounced different, maybe "Foock" or something else, surely not "Fuck"

One morning I was sitting at the counter sipping a chocolate ice cream soda. I liked to mix it up just a little and drink most of the soda and then eat the ice cream with the long handled spoon they give you. I had just taken a healthy sip of the soda when a man walked in and went over and picked up one of the papers. As he walked towards the counter to pay for the paper the pharmacist hollered from the back of the store.

"GOOD MORNING MR. FUCK."

I was amazed, I know you think I'm bullshitting you but I swear it's the honest truth. I tried googling the name recently to no avail but I suspect the family would have changed their name by now. This was back in the 60's and we were all a lot more innocent then.

1957 FORD HOT ROD (CAMP)

Well, not so much a hot rod per se, but damn powerful and fast either way. It belonged to my brother Bruce who still lived in Scranton. He wasn't using it anymore and we had it at the camp for hauling wood and stuff. The back seat was removed so we could put long logs in from the trunk. I used it in the evening to drive madly from one local town to the other near the camp looking for girls. I did this every evening rain or shine without fail. I never even saw a girl much less pick one up. Yet, hormones raging I kept at it. I guess the hunt is built into us. That would be fine but who was the ass who told the girls how desperate we always were. Their parents no doubt. Pity I didn't have at least one sister to clue me in. But alas, there I was driving at breakneck speed from town to town in the vain hunt for pussy.

I'd like to say that old age and lowered testosterone levels have abated that desire to hunt, to look, to hope. But it hasn't and now when a pretty girl smiles at me it stirs those old juices and makes me wonder if she's interested, but just for a moment. Then I realize that when a pretty young thing smiles at me it's more than likely I remind her of her grandfather.

Herkimer Street and Our First Landlord

Our first landlord on Herkimer Street was a real treat. I don't remember the husband much but the wife had a serious case of strange. Her one and only son inherited that trait from her. He was overweight and didn't like to go out. He'd stay in his room all day. The only time I saw him was when his mother would chase him out the front door and lock it. He would run around to the back door before she could get there to lock it and get back in. That was the only exercise he ever got.

They sold the house to a nice couple with a son just a couple years younger than me. Little John was a big kid for his age and went to St. Pats, a catholic school. He was taller than any of his classmates and the gym teacher thought he saw the makings of a basketball star in Little John. His Dad put a basketball hoop in the backyard and Little John practiced diligently. But at 14 and over six foot tall Little John was a hopeless klutz. Try as he might he could not get the hang of dribbling and running at the same time. For some odd reason he wore black leather shoes all the time too Even when he tried playing basketball in the back yard, which probably made the ball bounce further when he dribbled it off his toe. Something he did rather often I might add. He was a good guy and a friend even though I was always getting him in trouble with his parents.

I had all the makings of a drinking problem when with a large supply of beer I conned Little John into accompanying me down to his school for some trouble making. I drank a lot of the beer and I forgot why we went there when we did indeed get there. Undaunted, I climbed a tree in the little park opposite the school and talked Little John into climbing the other one. We stayed there for a while until my brother John, who had been told by someone where I was, came and got me … and Little John. Last I heard Little John was a cop, state cop I think. Seemed like a good match.

THE CLOSET BETWEEN MY BROTHERS BEDROOM AND MINE

When we lived on Herkimer Street in Syracuse there was a closet between my room and my brother Toms that we shared. If that wasn't bad enough Tom used the closet as a short cut to the bathroom through my bedroom. I protested in vain that he should take the long way around through the kitchen, dining room, then the bathroom. In desperation I moved my bed so that it blocked the closet door, that fixed him! Now when I needed to get in the closet I had to go around by way of the dining room, kitchen, HIS bedroom and then the closet. It wasn't perfect but I liked it.

I smoked back then and my favorite ashtray was this low crystal thing, looked expensive but it didn't hold much, still it had class. I also liked to read a lot, usually in bed. One day I was reading and smoking in bed while only wearing my skivvies. I set the cigarette on the ashtray that was next to me on the bed so I could turn the page of the book.

Out of the corner of my eye I saw the cigarette roll off the ashtray towards my scantly clad butt. With cat like reflexes I raised said butt to avoid the cigarette and with great force bashed my head on the doorknob to the closet. Stunned I sat back down … on the cigarette … which lined up perfectly with a large hole in my skivvies. My emergency mission quickly became getting my butt off that hot ash and I jumped out of bed clumsily knocking the night stand over. I turned my attention back to the bed and realized that the cigarette had burned through the sheet and was burning a hole in the foam mattress pad. In a panic I looked around for something to put out the fire and found … my hand! As I watched my hand moving towards the fire I knew that this was a bad idea but I just couldn't stop it in time.

After the fire was out and things had settled down I sat dazed on the floor amidst the mess, out of breath, trying to figure out which injury to rub first and what to rub it with.

The Search For Educational Materials

A friend of mine, Phil, actually he was a friend of my brother Tom, was really into naughty pictures … when he could get them. He must be in heaven now what with the Internet. His wife seemed to like it too but I never went into that much. One day he got a letter that simply said:

This is what you're looking for.

1 man 1 woman

2 men 1 woman

2 men 2 women

1 man 2 women

200 foot 8MM roll $40 your choice.

We studied the letter and discussed the various options to no end. He finally settled on, "2 men 2 women" as that, he reasoned, was the best value for the buck and sent away for it. A week or so later he called me and asked me to sneak my father's 8MM projector over to his house so we could watch it. I brought it over and he nervously loaded the film after taking a quick look at the first few feet.

"Look" he said as he held the film up to the light. Sure enough you could see 2 women and 2 men sitting on a couch.

"I bet they talk a little and then get naked and do it" Phil said.

We started the film and sure enough there they were sitting on the couch and talking … and talking … and talking.

Meanwhile Phil watched the film reel get smaller and smaller.

"They better start doing something soon or the film will run out" Phil said.

Then with just a few feet to go one of the girls got up and went down the hall followed by the camera.

"Now we got something" Phil said, as he glanced to see how much film was left.

The girl went into a room and closed the door, about a minute later, with just a few inches of film left, she opened the door and stuck her head out and tossed her blouse at the camera.

The End

Flashed on the screen…

Phil was beside himself with anger. I pointed out that they didn't lie to him in the letter, it was 2 men and 2 women.

"But they said it was what I was looking for" Phil said.

"I guess they thought you were looking for a movie about two men and two women sitting on the couch talking" I said.

I guess if there's a moral here it's be careful what you'r looking for, you might just get it. That sounds like the punch line to a joke. Phil, once burned, got what he was looking for later and amassed quite the naughty pictures collection.

One day he showed up with a worn deck of cards that I christened the, "Deck-O-Naughty Pictures." It was dog eared and faded but you could tell it was indeed naughty pictures. The country of origin was a subject of debate. I thought it was Mexico as the people were somewhat darker skinned. But these were printed cards of poor quality and hard to tell for sure. We sat and looked at the cards, oohing and awing until we'd get a card that was either so close up or faded that we couldn't tell who was doing what to whom. We would turn the cards around and around, hold them near and far but it was useless. There must have been at least 10 cards that were a mystery.

Most of what Phil got were black and white photographs. Naughty Pictures were very taboo and not sold in any stores. I bet you could buy drugs easier. But he got them somewhere. I particularly remember one very attractive woman, it may have been that Betty girl, the famous pinup girl. In this picture, not really naughty pictures, just completely nude, she was reclining on a divan with one leg up and one on the floor. It was from the side and you could not discern any detail in her crotch. Her pubic hair went from the usual place to her butt. As I had never seen one in real life at this point I thought they all looked like that. Hence the term, "Bush" I figured. She was a very hairy girl. I can still see her now in my minds eye.

Phil was a bit too obsessed with naughty pictures and several years older than me. We would sit at their coffee table looking at naughty pictures with his wife joining in. It was just too strange for me. As I look back at it now I wonder if she might have had different plans for me. I guess I'll just have to ponder that and fantasize about what might have been. She was a looker too and not many women like naughty pictures, or so I thought. I never met one besides her that did. More likely if they did like it they never told me. Hmm, maybe I should have asked. Who knows where that might have led. What strange alleys I could have gone down had I just asked the right question.

Are You a Beatnik?

I've always been close to clueless when it comes to girls. Now, in later life I'm still clueless. A woman damn near has to grab me by the balls before I realize she may want me. Oh well…

However, there has been a time or two when I did recognize an opportunity. Once when I was 16, I went up to the 'hill.' The hill is the SU hangout and surprise, it is on a hill. I guess the fancy names never make it when the obvious works. My reason for going to the hill was to try to pick up girls. At 16 this was damn near a lost cause. I was and remain eternally optimistic. Back then, and to this day, I am not a clothes horse. I had a deer skin suede jacket and the lining was shot but the leather was still good. It looked like a sport coat more than a jacket and its age and shabbiness added to its charm. I was also fond of moccasins then and had a pair that matched the jacket in style and comfort. To top the whole thing off I was not big on haircuts which may have been a throwback to a bad haircut, my mother, and a green plaid baseball cap that I was forced to wear one summer. However, I digress.

I was sitting in the Savoy restaurant on the hill nursing a coke, dressed in the above mentioned garb looking rather … shall we say unique. A rather fine looking young woman with her blonde hair done up in a beehive (popular in the 60's) took one look at me and asked me with a horny look in her eyes. "Are you a Beatnik?" "YES!" I said before having the time to think about it. She sat down and we went through the preliminaries one goes through before finding the true meaning for the back seat of my father's car. I found out later that she was also 16 and had come to the hill to find a college boy Beatnik to 'make it with' and she found me. She lived in Warners, NY about 20 miles from where I lived. One day when I didn't have the bus money or my father's car I went to her house on roller skates. My testosterone level was very high in those days.

Naturally I fell in love with her. A tendency I had for any woman who would let me play with her toys. They have so many you know and they all work just a little differently. Guys on the other hand have just the one and they all work pretty much the same. Girls are quite a bit more complex with erogenous zones and G-spots and such. One has to meander around the playing field trying to find the magic buttons to make them work. Maybe that's why boys play video games more than girls. Sort of a learning simulator for the vast unknown territory ahead. Dealing with girls wasn't easy when you have the ignorance of a 16 year old. I don't mean to imply that I've improved much with age. It's just that now I know I don't know what I'm doing. But somehow back then I muddled through and had a grand time.

So, armed with this new power, that of being a Beatnik, I became a Beatnik.

Reflecting on my life I am amazed at how the chief guiding thing, that thing that led me into adventure and trouble, that thing that got me where I am today ... was my dick.

Being a Beatnik got me laid a lot, but not as often as it could have if I had been aware of what women wanted of me. While my dick guided me, it didn't have a built in translator which would tell me what the subtle hints women gave off meant, that would have gotten me laid. Back in those days a woman practically had to come up to me, grab my dick and ask to get laid. But no, they were far more subtle than that and as a consequence I missed out on a lot of tail. For years I never knew I missed it. I would be watching TV or reading something when something came up that made me realize what "that girl" meant all those years earlier. I would often say to myself in times like these, "Damn! So that's what she meant! Son of a BITCH!" But it's too late for me now. I just hope that things like the Internet are providing help to clueless men like me and that the young men of today are making up for what I missed.

I INVENTED THE AIR GUITAR 50 YEARS AGO

There were some guys at one party who played in a band at Captain Mac's Clam Shack, the then current hangout for Syracuse University students. They didn't get paid but they got free beer. I asked if I could join them but I didn't play any instruments. I was enthusiastic and so they gave me a guitar and said I could pretend to strum it but I wasn't to hit any strings. I learned a few songs and off we went to "play." It worked great. I'm a fun drunk, just get me plastered and I'll sit in the corner and grin. All went well until I had a few beers and started hitting the strings and got kicked off the band.

So that's how I became a Beatnik… Worked well for me.

Towing the Cushman

I bought an old Cushman motor scooter for $20. I'd guess it was a 1947 or so. Painted green with a brush and quite a bit of rust. It ran but I didn't have plates on it so Tom suggested I could drive it legally if he "towed" me with John's scooter. We rigged up a rope about the length of the scooters and got ready to try it out.

"You'll have to brake me so when I signal, put on your brakes and stop us both." He said

Okay, that sounded reasonable so off we went. Both scooters puttering along until Tommy signaled for me to stop. I put the brake pedal to the floor and not much happened. Maybe it slowed down but it was never going to stop us both, maybe not even me alone. Tom had to stop so he applied his brake and I turned to the right to miss him but just as I got even with him the rope tightened up, we came together and my scooter turned over on top of him and John's scooter. Nobody got hurt but he sure was pissed. It wasn't as if I didn't try to stop. I just never checked the brakes. I assumed they worked. The motor ran and that's all I cared about.

I didn't have the money to fix the brakes or the plates or any of that stuff. When I bought it I thought of none of those things. It sat in the garage for a while until I sold it for what I paid for it.

The Cushman was an interesting scooter. It was referred to as the cow catcher because of the way the back looked. The engine looked like the ones they used in old washing machines with a kick starter in the center, not like motorcycles which have it on the side. You would pick the pedal up till it caught and kicked down. Then reach down again and repeat. Very crude. The floor where you sat was flat. The cylinder head was just under the seat with the spark plug pointing forward at a 45 degree angle. Good thing there was a thick seat mounted on a hinged piece of plywood or you'd fry you nuts with the spark plug.

I told you that to tell you this. (Ron Thomason etc)

Some time later I was riding John's scooter at Split Rock, an old quarry out in the country. Many years before this a fireworks factory exploded there. I often wondered exactly where it was, as there was nothing remaining of it. I met another kid riding a Cushman just like the one I had and we decided to ride together. His wasn't licensed so we had to stay within the quarry area. It was perhaps 100 acres or so and there were plenty of places to ride. Plus he said he lived close by and only had to cross the road once to get home. We rode for a bit and then we came up on a shallow stream with me riding ahead and I just stood up and let the scooter ride the rough stream bed. He held back so I stopped.

"What's a matter," I said?

"I'm not sure I can do that." He said

"Sure you can, just stand up and it'll be easy." I said.

He took my advice and started to cross the creek with the Cushman bouncing underneath. I tried to warn him but it was too late or he was too far away to hear me but as the Cushman bounced up and down in the rough stream bed the seat he had, which was not attached with a hinge like my old one, bounced off into the creek. He didn't realize it and once past the creek he sat down on the head of the motor and the spark plug's thousands of volts got him in the nuts. From where I was watching all I could see was him with both arms and legs straight out like he was doing a jumping jack and the Cushman going on a ways without him until it tipped over. He reminded me of the wolf in the Road Runner cartoons.

I went back and found him laying on his side in a fetal position holding his nuts with both hands and groaning.

"Shit man, I'm sorry, I didn't know your seat wasn't attached." I said.

He just looked at me as if he was holding his breath and his bulging eyes got all watery and the grimace on his face was terrible to see. I didn't know what to do so I did that … nothing. After a bit the pain seemed to ease and he started looking better and finally he got up and limped to where his seat was in the creek, put it on his Cushman, forded the creek walking by the scooter and went home.

I often wonder if that shocking experience affected him in his later life. Could he have children for example? Guess I'll never know.

Sure I Know How to Ride, I Assured the Pretty Blond Girl...

Truth is I never rode a horse in my life but she was so damn pretty and looked so sexy as they rode up to the White Birch Camp that evening. I was there to help my Dad cut trees for firewood for the hunting season. He had guns and stuff but he never really hunted in my lifetime. He just liked going out into the woods and cutting trees up for firewood, and he rarely cut live trees

We were working on some things in the yard when two girls rode up on horses. This was odd for several reasons. It was the first time anyone came to the camp on horseback and it was the first time one much less two girls came to the camp for any reason.

The blonde about my age was very pretty, a real beauty, the other girl was her younger sister and of no interest to me. I had driven by their house a hundred times on my way too and from the camp and never saw either one of them. My guess is their Dad probably kept them hidden. We talked for a bit and then the one my age, Debbie said.

"Do you ride?" I assumed she meant horses so I said, "Yes, sure, a lot."

"Why don't you stop by after dinner and we'll take a nice evening ride?" She said.

"Sure, what time?" I said.

"How about 7." She said.

"I'll be there." I said.

They left and I must say that a pretty girl in tight jeans with a blond pony tail riding away from you on a horse is a sweet sight to see.

"Have you ever ridden a horse before?" My Dad asked.

"Yeah, sure, down on the farm, remember." I said.

"That horse bucked you off before you got two feet." He said.

"No, I rode it from the barn to the gate to the field and then it bucked me off." I said.

"Your cousin was holding the reins until you got to the gate." He said.

Point taken, but I had a plan. Did I mention how pretty she was?

I arrived at their farm at the end of the road leading to the camp about 6:30 and knocked on the door.

"You're early, we haven't finished dinner yet, come on in." Her Mom said.

"I'm sorry to be early, I'll go wait in the barn and look at the horses." I said.

"Okay, suit yourself, they're in that barn over there." She said as she pointed to the barn across the road.

I went across the road to where the horses were and started talking to them.

"Look, I really like this girl and want to make a good impression on her so if you guys would help me out I'd appreciate it." I said as I gave each of them a carrot I brought with me. I stroked their heads and did everything I could to ingratiate myself with them.

Hey, I said I had a plan, I didn't say it was a good one.

Debbie came out after dinner and asked me which horse I liked. I realize now that she knew I didn't know horses but she was trying to be kind.

"I like this one." I said pointing to the one who looked the most friendly.

"She's a bit head strong, you may be better off with this one." She said pointing to another one. "She's gentle and easier to ride." She said.

"No, that's okay, this one will be fine." I said. I couldn't let her think I needed a gentle horse.

I tried to help her saddle the horses as it became increasingly obvious that I didn't know what I was doing.

"You sure you want that horse?" She asked yet again.

"Sure as can be." I said bravely.

I managed to get on the horse and not look like a complete jerk and we started down the road in the direction of the camp which was 2 miles away. Then after a bit just when I thought I had a handle on this horse riding thing Debbie took off in a gallup. Apparently my horse took this as a challenge and did not like losing and we took off in hot pursuit, caught up with them, passed them at great speed and kept on going. Nothing I tried would slow that damn horse down so I just held on and waited for the end to come. I watched the rough rocks in the road flashing by and visions of flying through the air like down at the farm filled me with dread. My horse got tired after what seemed like forever and slowed down enough to let Debbie catch up with us, grabbed the reins and brought us to a stop.

"You really don't ride do you." She asked the obvious question.

"Well, I didn't fall off." I said.

She laughed and we walked the horses back to the barn. Just idle chit chat with me humbled and trying to be honest.

"I really like you." I said. "How about I take you out to a movie or maybe dinner." I said.

"Why not both." She said.

"Great." I said. "When would you like to go? I asked.

"It will have to be tomorrow as I'm going home the day after." She said.

"I thought you lived here on the farm." I said.

"No, I'm just visiting my aunt and uncle, I live in Philadelphia." She said.

I was very disappointed, I thought this was the beginning of something. I come down here every summer and Thanksgiving and I hoped I could see her more.

"That's too bad." I said. "What time tomorrow?"

"How about 5 and we can make a big evening of it." She said.

"Five it is." I said.

Pop wasn't happy. He wanted to work most of the day and I wanted to quit at 3 so I could get ready. He also wasn't happy when I hit him up for $20 for my date. But he realized I was next to worthless anyway because all I could think about was Debbie. He reluctantly relented and we quit at 3. I preened and prepped and at quarter to 5 I headed out for our date.

Debbie was beautiful, perhaps the most beautiful girl I had ever met, and she was sweet and considerate too. She and I both knew I was new at this. I never asked but I'm sure she had a couple years on me and I was barely 17. We went to a nice restaurant and a movie in town afterwards. I was in heaven and didn't want the date to end. I drove back as slow as the car would go. Good thing it was a country road with almost no traffic. Back at her place we sat in the car for a bit and talked about a million things. I figured the more I talked the longer the evening would last. We kissed a couple of times and it was as sweet as I imagined it would be. Why did she have to leave tomorrow? Just when I found her I lose her.

"I'll come down in the morning and see you off." I said.

"No, don't do that. It's better we say goodbye now. Besides we'll be leaving very early and my uncle will be mad if we're delayed." She said.

"Okay." I said.

We talked some more, kissed some more, held hands some more. When she went in I was sick to my stomach with the dread of losing her.

I never heard from her again. We didn't exchange addresses, we couldn't write. She didn't tell me when or if she'd be at the farm again so I was never going to see her again. It made me very sad. I drove Pop's car slowly back down the dirt road we had ridden the day before, reliving that ride and the walk back. I could still feel her lips on mine, smell her perfume, feel her presence. I had fallen in love with her.

But I got over it.

I always did.

I am a sucker for a pretty girl, putty in their hands, a fool for love. Or just a fool. Over the years I've learned one thing and that is there are lots and lots of pretty girls and I did my damnedest to fall in love with each and every one of them.

You Can't Make a Move on a Girl in a TR-3

My brother Tom bought a 1958 Triumph TR-3 with my father co-signing for the loan. Everything went along fine for some time. Tom had his own ideas about how the car worked. For example, he considered the tachometer's red line, the amount of revs the engine was turning over, to be an indication of peak efficiency and not something to be wary of. We were driving back from Scranton to Syracuse about 4 miles south of Binghamton, NY on route 81and going much past the red line when very loudly:

BANG BANG BANG BANG BANG BANG BANG
BANG BANG BANG BANG BANG BANG BANG
BANG BANG BANG BANG BANG BANG BANG
BANG BANG BANG BANG BANG BANG BANG
BANG BANG BANG BANG

Tom pulled over to the side of the road and left the engine running. It was loud, very loud. Tom raised the hood.

"Sounds like a lifter came loose" He said.

I know what a lifter is and there was no way a lifter could be making that kind of noise.

"I think you threw a rod." I said. Yelling over the racket the engine was making.

"No, it's a lifter I'm sure." He said

We got back into the car and drove the four miles to a garage. I was sure the damn thing was going to blow up and told Tom so. He ignored me, I was his little brother and he knew more than I did. As we were coming down the exit ramp a good ways from the garage the mechanic came out and watched us come in, it was that loud.

"Can I borrow some tools to get the valve cover off, a lifter came loose?" Tom said.

"That ain't no lifter, you blew a rod." The mechanic said.

Tom insisted it was a lifter and again asked to borrow some tools. The mechanic shrugged and motioned towards the tools and went back to work. Tom took the valve cover off but couldn't find a loose lifter.

"I guess I blew a rod" He said.

The mechanic sighed and looked to the sky, we exchanged knowing glances and he went back to his work.

It couldn't be fixed there so my Dad had it towed back to Syracuse. Of course they had to remove the engine to fix it and that entailed removing the entire front of the car. I stopped by to check on the progress and was shocked to see it so far apart. I remember it cost $450 dollars, that's 1961 dollars which is probably ten times that now.

I don't remember who had to come up with the $450 but it was probably my Dad. I don't think Tom had that kind of money. I know I didn't. I was working part time at the Grand Union supermarket in Westvale making about $45 a week. The assistant manager didn't like me for some reason, probably too arrogant or a wise ass or something like that. He wanted me to quit and gave me one shitty job after another. One day he decreed that the upstairs toilet needed to be cleaned and that I should do it.

The upstairs was the warehouse where the supplies came in They were sent down to the floor by a conveyor belt. This was mostly done at night when the store was closed. The assistant manager showed me the restroom in the back of the warehouse in a corner. It was gross. Two stalls, two urinals, a couple sinks in a room with ceramic tiles on the walls and floor. There was a floor drain in the middle of it all. There was a large hot water heater just outside the door. He told me to get what cleaning supplies I needed from the stock on the floor and showed me where the mop and other stuff is. He expected it would take me the rest of my shift to clean it and said not to come back downstairs until it sparkled.

After he left I hunted around for supplies and collected them together. There was an old heavy green rubber hose near the hot water heater which gave me an idea. With "No Time For Sergeants" fresh in my mind, I smiled a wry smile and chuckled a bit as I proceeded.

Frist I cranked up the temperature on the hot water to it's highest setting. Then I took all the paper products out of the bathroom and put them outside. I then opened all the paper towel holders and everything else. I opened the window to air things out. Hose in hand I sprayed down the entire room ceiling to floor with hot steaming water. Then I sprayed and splashed a lot of cleaning fluid over everything and sprayed it down again. It was hard to see with the steam and all so I would do a little and then stop. By the time I was finished that bathroom was cleaner than when it was new and I didn't have to get my hands dirty.

I sat outside and read some magazines I had found. They were out of date and destined to be returned to the publisher. When everything dried out inside I went back in and wiped down all the chrome to remove the water spots which didn't take long. Then I put all the paper back in, turned the hot water temp back to where it was, put the hose back and spent the rest of my shift reading. The whole thing took less than an hour. But I knew it was too soon to get the assistant manager because he had to be kept thinking I was doing this shitty job for hours and hours. My biggest problem was boredom. About 5 minutes before my shift was up I heard him coming up the steps to check on me. I did a quick look around to make sure everything was in place and with a rag in hand I awaited his arrival.

He scowled at me as he approached,

"You finished with that?" He said.

"Yes sir." I said.

While wringing my hands with the rag. He gave me a sour look and opened the door with me following and walked to the middle of the room.

"How the fuck did you get this this clean?" He said.

"I just scrubbed and scrubbed until it was done. I just finished as you were coming up the stairs." I said.

"Harumph." He grunted. "Quitting time, get out of here." He mumbled.

I had outsmarted him and he never knew that I spent most of my shift laying on food supply boxes doing nothing but reading magazines.

Everyone was very impressed with the job I did and no one but me knew how I did it. I didn't get fired and the assistant manager stopped taunting me. He stopped giving me crappy jobs and we were both happier about the whole thing.

I don't know if there's a moral here or not. But by doing more than was expected and a better job than anyone else could have done I learned a good lesson. Perhaps it's that old saying, "Don't let the bastards get you down."

I told you that to tell you this. (Again that's from Ron Thomason)

Tom was having his own troubles with the TR-3. He didn't make enough to make the payments and do the maintenance on the car. He came to an agreement with Pop where Pop took the car back from Tom and it sat parked in the back yard for two weeks. Meanwhile my mother was working at the SU hospital so my other brother John could get a break on tuition and get his EE degree. She would go to work at 8 and come home at 4 and she did this by bus. I always had a certain kind of game I played with my Dad. I would try to con him out of something by being clever and he would enjoy it. So, I bided my time and when it looked good I suggested the plan that I had formulated. Tom wasn't there or he would have objected I'm sure.

"Pop." I said. "Mom goes to work at 8 and comes home at 4."

"Um huh." He said looking at me wondering what scheme I had up my sleeve.

"She has to go on the bus and that takes a lot of time."
I said.

"Uh huh." He said watching me very closely now.

"I go to school at 9 and come home at 3." I said.

"Uh huh." He said and I think he could see where I was going with this.

"I could drive Mom to work in the TR-3 and be back here in plenty of time to get to school and then I would be home in time to go get her when she got off of work at 4." I said.

The key to this plan's success is that I would only be using the TR-3 to help Mom and not myself.

He leaned back in his chair and chewed on his food and looked at me. I think I detected a slight smile as he realized he was trapped.

"Okay, but you come right back here after you take her and you don't drive anywhere else." He said.

"Of course, that's all I want to do." I said.

Part B of my plan only took two more weeks. Every day I would do exactly as we agreed. I would get up early and drive Mom to work, come back home and walk to school. Then after school I would come home, get the TR-3 and pick Mom up. I never varied from the agreed upon plan. After about two weeks I timed it perfectly when I would do Part B. It was as before at dinner. We were finishing up, just Pop, Mom and I when I laid it all out.

"Pop, when I drive Mom to work I drive right by my school and when I pick her up after work I drive by my school again. It would save gas if I just drove her to work, went to school and picked her up after school." I said.

He leaned back in his chair and I knew he was trying to hide a smile. My logic was impeccable, the car was here, he had to pay for it anyway and it was better for it to be driven than just sit there. He must have know Part B was coming because he had his own plan.

"Okay, but you pay for all the gas and maintenance, I'll keep paying the loan payment." He said.

"You got a deal." I said happily.

It had taken me just 4 weeks to work this deal and I had a car! But not just a car, it was a cool sports car and no one in my class at school even had a car of any sort. I was king of the road.

One problem…

That damn thing required a lot of maintenance, more than I could make at the Grand Union. Every penny I had went into it. I found ways to make a few extra bucks. On school days after dropping my Mom off I would drive around to the bus stops and pick kids up in exchange for that twenty-five cents bus fare which would buy a gallon of gas in those days. You'd be surprised how many kids you can fit in a TR-3 with the top down.

Back to the original reason for telling you this. First you need to know the layout of a TR-3. It's small. Both the drivers and passenger seats are on the floor with your feet almost straight in front of you. It's not easy to get into, kinda like getting into a small barrel. The hump between the seats is high with the heater on top with vents blowing to each side. In the winter my right leg would be on fire while my left froze. It was so low to the ground that all the cars in front of you covered the windshield with crap.

No windshield washer either. I had to leave the side flap loose and carry a spray can of Windex, reach my hand out the window and spray it at almost every stop. It was so low to the ground that clumps of ice that dropped off other cars would sometimes get lodged under it. It started so hard on cold mornings that I would get up early and go out and light charcoal in a flat pan, go back inside and wait a bit and then put the pan under the oil pan. It's amazing it didn't catch fire. The seats were true bucket seats that held you in place during hard driving and everything else.

I took a girl on a date and afterwards we went parking. That was a waste of time. I couldn't even get a little boob and a kiss was barely possible. I swore at the time that if I ever had a daughter I would feel safe with her going out with a guy driving a TR-3. You truly can't make a move on a girl in one of those damn things, even if she wanted you too.

The Party To End All Parties

My parents were going away for a week and I was left to fend for myself. Shouldn't be a problem, I was 16 or 17 and all grown up. When my friends found out I had a whole house to myself they decreed that I should have a party, a big party. Word got out on the hill about this big party and I got very concerned. I'd lost control of events, people knew me and it was expected of me that I would not pass up this opportunity for the big party.

My house, actually the bottom floor of a two family house consisted of a front room where my Mom kept her piano, the middle room right at the front entrance, the dining room and then the kitchen. The three bedrooms were to the left side as you came in the front door with the bathroom between the second and third bedrooms. Mine was the second and my brother Tom's was third at the back next to the kitchen.

People started arriving early and it quickly became apparent that something had to give. We moved all the furniture to the front room and I took up the carpet in the dining room and decreed that that was the room that all the drinking would take place. I left the pad which was an odd product my father was selling. It was a carpet pad with a printed top. The idea was you could use it as a carpet for a while and then as a pad later. We used it as a pad. So the setup for the party was the entrance room, dining room and kitchen.

More and more kids arrived, each one bringing a case of beer as that was the admittance fee. It soon became apparent that our small refrigerator would not hold it all. At least not with all the food my parents left me for the week.

So they ate the food, took all the shelves out of the refrigerator and stacked the bottles of Topper beer until the thing was full. I tried to keep the noise down because the landlord lived upstairs and came down a few times to scold me about what I was up to. What could I do, I couldn't kick all those people out and to be honest I was having a good time and feeling like, "The Man" who threw the biggest party that would be talked about for months afterwards. It went on all night and well into the next day. People left and came back and new people showed up throughout the day.

By the evening it was over. There were several people who kinda 'moved in' and were sleeping on the floor. I got pissed when I found a couple having sex on my mom's bed as I had ruled her bedroom out of bounds. Other than that things went pretty good. I got hungry. They ate all my food and my parents wouldn't be back for days and I had no money. So we took the empty Topper beer bottles back and bought food with the deposit. Not much, just enough to get by. I bet I must have lost weight but maybe not. Beer is a food after all and I had a lot of that. A couple days before my parents came home some friends came over, I don't think they really left. Anyway, we cleaned up the house.

The rug/pad in the dining room was soaked with beer, there was no cleaning it. I gave it to Kitty where it would fit right in to her apartment which was already soaked in beer and lots of other liquids that I'll leave to your imagination. I worried my parents would discover the pad missing but what could I do. We cleaned and scrubbed and put furniture back until the house looked as it did before the party. Or so I thought. I spent the entire day before my parents returned going over the house top to bottom and I thought I had it.

I was wrong.

When my parents came back the first thing they noticed was the almost empty refrigerator. Then my father walked across the dining room carpet, stopped, had a odd look in his eye, bent over and lifted the corner of the carpet and asked,

"I thought there was a pad under this?" He said.

I played innocent,

"No. it's always been like that." I said.

With a questioning look he walked away but the buzzards were circling. I made it through the night and by the next day I thought I had pulled it off. That is until my mother reached behind the heavy table in the dining room we didn't move and fished out a Topper beer bottle cap,

"What's this?" She asked me.

"Looks like a bottle cap." I said.

"We don't drink Topper beer here." She said.

"Umm," I mumbled, thinking silence was my only recourse. But she was hot on the trail and scoured the house as only a mother can and found little things here and there. The evidence mounted and I had this sinking feeling, much like that of a condemned man on his way to the gallows. I still protested my innocence as best I could but I forgot about the landlord upstairs. My father came in and set me down.

"Tell me what happened?" he demanded.

"I don't know what you're talking about." I said.

"I just talked to the landlord." He said, and sat there staring at me, waiting.

Crap! The jig was up and there was no use trying to deny it anymore. But I shrunk the truth. Most people would stretch the truth but I shrunk it.

I said, "Okay, I had a small party with just a few friends and we had some beer."

Hell I was almost old enough to drink legally. That didn't faze him.

"What happened to the pad?" He said.

He sat there with the confidence of a man who knew the truth, the whole truth and he was just playing a game with me to see if I could talk my way out of this.

I said, "I have this girlfriend Kitty, who lives on the hill and she doesn't have a carpet in her apartment and the floor is cold and I felt sorry for her and besides we spilled a little beer on it and it smelled bad."

"Wouldn't Kitty mind the smell?" He said.

Normally he would have had me there but I came back with,

"No, because her apartment is in an old house and the whole house smells so bad you can't notice it." I said.

(Crap, we could have wrung that pad out and got a few more bottles of beer out of it.)

"Besides I know you wouldn't have wanted it after we spilled the beer on it and I thought I was doing a good deed where everyone won … wasn't I?" I said innocently while looking him straight in the eye.

"Hmm." He said and wandered off.

I thought I had pulled it off...

But my mother, who could have worked for CSI, hell she could have run the place, wasn't done.

"Why did you wash the sheets on my bed?" She said innocently during dinner.

I had tried my best to make up the bed like she did but as any guy will tell you we are incapable of making up a bed that good. She had me and I knew it but I wasn't giving up quite yet.

"I slept in there while I washed the sheets on my bed." I said.

"Why didn't you sleep in Tom's bed?" she asked sweetly?

"Tom's bed, you wouldn't catch me dead in Tom's bed!" I said strongly.

"Hmm." She said.

Tag teaming me they were. A technique they obviously perfected after having four boys all older than me.

"How many people were at your party?" Pop asked.

I could answer this one without lying.

"I don't know for sure, they were coming and going and I wasn't keeping count." I said. Hell, that was really true.

"Must have been a hell of a lot of people here if you could't keep count." He said.

Shit! I should have thought that one through before answering, what to say, what to say.

"I spent most of my time in the kitchen seeing after my guests and couldn't keep track." I said.

Would that fly? Not really because they both knew what had gone on, they talked to the landlord. They were just playing with me, trying to catch me in an obvious lie but I knew the limits of this game. I could stretch the truth, maybe not tell them everything but if I outright lied that would be a disaster.

Then the idiot hit the fan. One of my not very close friends, who assumed my parents knew and approved of my party came over and said in front of me AND my parents.

"Boy, that was one heck of a party you guys had, I'll bet there was a hundred people here, cars were parked all the way up and down the street and it went on for at least two days." He said.

If I only had one of my fathers guns I would have shot the bastard dead, then and there!

My parents just looked at me. No expression, no emotion, they just stared at me. I decided to hang with my friend silence for a while. The idiot left once he realized he had let the cat out of the bag. So there I was, in my room, reading a book as I usually did. My father knocked on the door.

"Come in." I said.

He came in a few feet and looked down at me.

"You think we didn't know?" He asked.

"That's what I was hoping for." I said.

"Was it really that big?" He asked.

"Yup, they're still talking about on the hill and it's a week later." I said.

He tried to hide the smile while he turned his head away.

"You owe me for that pad." He said.

"Yes sir." I said.

That smile told me something. He was proud of me but I wasn't sure why. Years later, with the experience age brings, I realized he was kinda reliving his youth through me. Many years later he brought it up at the camp and bragged about the party his son had that the kids talking about for months. It makes me feel good today to know he was proud of me. A pride I'm sure would have vanished if I out and out lied to him. It wasn't the first time I made him proud and it wasn't the last but it was the last party I had at our house.

PS I never did repay him for the pad. I didn't have any money you know. But I still owe him … a lot.

Captain Jack's Clam Shack

Once I became a Beatnik I started to go to parties on The Hill at various Beatnik's apartments. We sat around and listened to folk music and mused about the meaning of life. There wasn't many drugs back then. Peyote and uppers, Dexedrine I think. Those little yellow pills that kept you up all night. One night I was given several of them and I was amazed at how their effect showed me the true meaning of life. I wanted to make sure I didn't forget it so I spent the evening writing it all down. It was such a revelation. The next day I awoke and wanted to review the brilliant findings from the night before... Gibberish, it was just gibberish! It made no sense and I realized the true meaning of life still eluded me and the folly of taking those drugs.

Peyote was a lot more fun once you got past swallowing it. That took dedication as it was so bad you wanted to throw up. I managed to get down one peyote bud and the hallucinations were a lot of fun. Every time I see some dazzling computer graphics today it takes me back to that night. No need for peyote now, just turn on your screen saver and you'll get the same effect without throwing up. My drug imbibing was pretty much over, although I did try pot twice and didn't care for it. The last time I took pot I overdid it and for several days after I would suddenly break out laughing at the most inappropriate times. I didn't like that loss of control and never took it again. I prefer reality to whatever drugs give you.

Captain Jack was a neat guy and he gave me a job as a clam husker in the shack side of the operation. By then he had expanded the shack into a restaurant next door. The shack still operated as a clam shack serving clams, lobster, fish sandwiches and chips. I got proficient at husking clams but soon realized my skin was allergic to clam juice so I became the cook. I did stemmed clams, fried fish and chips and whatever else was called for in the small kitchen that also served as a hallway between the shack and the restaurant.

One evening as they were wont to do, some girl tried to flush a Kotex down the ladies room toilet and Jack called me to get the snake and unclog it as it was the only toilet the gals had. The ladies john was to the right of the stage and the only way to get there was by walking down between the tables in the dining room. As I walked carrying the snake a cheer went up from the girls which embarrassed the hell out of me. I knocked on the door to make sure it was empty and went in and unclogged the toilet, rinsed off the snake and came out to more cheers which embarrassed me even more.

As I walked up the aisle holding the snake at arms length a girl stood up, grabbed me and french kissed me while I was holding the damn thing. Turns out she knew me from the neighborhood and had the hots for me and not for some time in the future, but right then and there! Susan, the head waitress was all for enhancing my love life. She was dating a black guy which was all the fashion in the 60's and I assumed she knew of what she spoke. She suggested that the large roof of the beer cooler would be an appropriate place to do the deed.

The beer cooler was outside and accessed through a door that was conveniently right next to the table where the girl sat waiting for me. So, knowing full well that everyone in the dining room knew was happening I walked over to her and grabbed her by the hand and out the door we went to cheers from the crowd. Oh hell, what could be more embarrassing. We climbed up on the metal cooler's roof which I incorrectly assumed would be metal like the rest of the cooler. It wasn't, it was gravel on tar. So, now what. It didn't bother the girl any and she dropped her pants and lay down and spread herself waiting for my arrival. I dropped my pants to my knees and using the bunched up pants as a cushion, I got on with it. It was the least romantic screw I ever had, much like two dogs fucking in the parking lot. But it scratched the itch we both had.

Afterwards we lay there looking at the stars, It was really overcast and all we saw were grey clouds. Anyway, stars sounds a little more romantic. So, we lay there looking at the stars and talked about things in the neighborhood and how she always wanted to fuck me. I guess I was on her bucket list before bucket lists were invented. Now that we fucked she didn't want to pursue any kind of relationship. I was kinda sad about that because girls that french kiss like her and will fuck on a beer cooler roof are hard to come by.

The beer cooler was a good sized affair. It was a walk in cooler, probably about 8 feet wide by 12 feet long and as I said, made of metal. The beer was kept at an approximate temperature that was near to ideal but not perfect. The cooler in the shack held 6 kegs, 3 of each type of beer we sold. One a dark ale and the other a regular beer. The cooler in the bar was exactly right on temperature and as a keg was emptied it was rolled out through the dining room to sit next to the beer cooler and a new one brought in. This was done so the new keg would have a chance to get to the exact temperature. So, you may wonder why this is important.

If the beer is too warm it will create a big head which customers won't like. The bartender would then pour the beer down the side of the glass to make up for that. This is wrong too as beer should be poured down the middle of the glass so it can release the carbon dioxide that makes the head. By pouring beer down the side of the glass or drinking it direct from the bottle that gas is released in your stomach, which is why beer drinkers belch a lot. When bartenders pour a jug of beer they will pour it down the side to keep the gas in the beer till the customer pours it in a glass himself. If they poured it down the middle the beer would get flat fast. Now that you know that hint let me give you another.

How do you tell if your glass is clean? If you see bubbles on the inside side of the glass then the glass isn't clean. It's not dirty, it just has residue, soap whatever on it that reacts to the beer causing the bubbles. Bars use a special soap that's supposed to reduce that but you almost never get a completely clean glass. Beer aficionados will use the first glass of beer to 'clean' the glass and ask the bartender to just refill that rather than get a new one. So, some things to impress your date with next time you have one.

THE SUMMER OF DEX

One day I was sitting on Kitty's roof. She had a second floor apartment and her living room window gave access to the porch roof that was almost flat. The landlord was an old guy in his 90's I think. He was deaf which was a godsend with an apartment house full of Beatniks. There I was on the roof in the middle of a sunny day watching the world go by when an acquaintance named John came screaming down Crouse Ave in his convertible with the top down. I didn't know John very well, not even sure his name was John for that matter, but John it will be for the sake of this story. John was shit faced drunk and ran up on the curb almost hitting a parked car and blowing out his right front tire.

This all happened right across the street in front of me. I went down to help him change the tire before the cops arrived. He was so wasted he was of little help, hell all he did was put the key in the trunk lock and couldn't even turn it to open it. So I sat him down in the car and changed the tire. John thanked me profusely, reached down to a box sitting on the passenger floor marked, "Hubble Drugs," grabbed a quart sized brown bottle and gave it to me and went on his merry way. After I watched him weave down the street out of sight and didn't hear a crash I looked at the bottle. "1000 Dexedrine"

HOLY FUCK!

The narcs were everywhere and damn easy to spot by the way. Apparently they weren't up to the art of undercover work back then and it was easy to spot a suit in a sea of raggedy jeans. Anyway, I shit my pants when I realized what I had. This was enough uppers to put me away for life for Chris's sake. I didn't want them but I didn't not want them either. I carried them back to Kitty's apartment and hid them ... and then hid them again ... and again. I must have hid them a dozen times. It felt like the narcs were about to come pounding on the door at any moment.

What happened if John got pulled over and spilled it that he had given me these drugs. I was freaking out. It took hours for me to calm down and when the gang got back I told them about it. There were perfectly fine that I keep them and dole out a few when they wanted them but not one of them wanted to hold onto them either. We were brainwashed back then and having drugs just wasn't a very common occurrence. One of the gang, Jake, a really weird guy with bulging eyes was into every drug there was. He bought the book, "Psychedelic Review" I think it was and read it cover to cover.

Kitty's boyfriend, if you could call him that because all of us screwed Kitty at one time or another. She was kinda the groups lay. Anyway Brian was cool and really smart. Jake was reading the SU College paper about a special tree Syracuse University just received as a gift and it was somehow special. Jake was looking in his book and was thinking the tree might be the one in the book. It had a unique bark that would get you high if you made tea from it. Brian looked at the book and said he thought it was. He was just bullshitting Jake but Jake took him seriously. The next day we got word that the campus police had arrested Jake for vandalism to the tree. Turns out he was up there late at night shaving pieces of bark off the tree!

When he got out he pleaded with me to come with him to the tree. As we casually walked by we could see the bark he had shaved off. He cajoled me into going over and picking up the bark he had shaved off. We were both nervous because this was in the quad and there were people everywhere. So as stealthily as I could, I would wonder over by the tree and drop something and pick it and some of the bark from the ground. I'd wonder around a bit and end up back by Jake and hand off the bark to him. It was like spy stuff in the movies with two of the worst spies ever. This took a couple of hours and I was absolutely sure we were being watched but we got away with it. I knew the bark was bullshit and told Jake so. Told him Brian was pulling his leg but he had convinced himself that this bark was 'the' bark that would get him high.

Later, back at Kitty's he used the bark and brewed up some tea. It smelled bad and no one else wanted any part of it. We were all pretty much drug free and didn't even have money for beer. So we watched Jake drink the awful tasting tea. Nobody else tasted it but from the look of Jakes face it must have been awful. Brian encouraged Jake. He sat there looking like he was reading the book and telling Jake some of what he should feel.

"I think I'm feeling something." Jake would say as he sipped that god awful brew.

"I think I'm feeling something now." He said.

Meanwhile Brian just kept pretending to read the book and feed Jake line after bullshit line about what a wonderful high he was going to get.

"I think I'm feeling it now." Jake said and sipped more tea.

Hours went by with Brian reading the book, Jake sipping the tea and the rest of us just enjoying the show. One thing I'll never forget from this experience. Druggies are really stupid. Hours later when Jake could no longer, "Feel anything" he said. "I don't think that was the right tree. Maybe it's somewhere else on campus." And off he went in search of the holy high. We didn't see him for days.

CHERRY BOMBS AND SLINGSHOTS

I had a Wham-O slingshot and Brian had some cherry bombs. We sat in Kitty's apartment and the idea came to us that we could lob a cherry bomb from the porch roof to the intersection of Crouse and Marshall Street, a block or so away and no one would know where it came from. It took a few tries but we finally got the trajectory just right. We waited for dark...

Marshall street is the main drag for SU kids. There are restaurants and shops there and everyone hung out there. It was prestigious to have a second floor apartment overlooking Marshall Street, some even had balconies. When it got dark we started lobbing cherry bombs. They exploded in the air about 20 feet off the ground, most of them anyway. We shot the first off and waited... Nothing. Sent another and another, always waiting 10 minutes or so between shots. Then, though the trees we saw the police in their cruiser talking to students on the corner. We're over a block away so we couldn't hear what they were saying. When they got back in their cruiser we shot off another cherry bomb. Out they popped and stayed longer each time. More cruisers showed up and we waited till things calmed down and when they were about to leave we set another cherry bomb on it's way.

The cops were convinced someone on the roof or the balcony was setting them off and soon we saw them on the balcony taking to kids. It got heated at times. We just sat on the roof and watched. We were running low on cherry bombs so we waited to have the greatest effect. Besides the cops were there in force by now and stayed at least a half hour before they started to leave. Once they got back in their cars I loaded another bomb and Brian said to wait a bit more. We waited until there was just one cop car left and Brian said, "Now" lit the fuse and I let her fly.

My shot couldn't have been more accurate or just dumb luck as the previous ones were going off all over the place. This one went off about 5 feet above the cop car's roof and man did that bring out the troops. We decided that caution was the better part of valor and retreated back into the apartment. We watched through the window as a large number of cops converged on the area. There was even one at the corner just a few feet from where we were. We discussed whether we should set off another bomb because the cops could see the trail of sparks from the fuse. Back then we thought cops had more savvy than I do now and we didn't have the balls to pursue it. It was the talk of the street for days afterwards and the cops were really pissed so we couldn't even brag about it. Ah, the good old days of fun, frolic and causing innocent mayhem.

BACK TO THE 1,000 PILLS

Dexedrine is an upper. It keeps you awake for hours and seems to give you energy you didn't have. When the pill wears off it's a downer. You need lots of sleep. Kids use it to stay awake for tests and doctors, nurses and truckers use it to keep alert for long shifts.

I had that bottle of pills for months. Eventually I transferred them to a brown paper bag, thinking somehow they would be less illegal that way. I then hid them on the shelf over the mens toilet at the Clam Shack. The men's john was just behind the kitchen where I worked and was off the hallway the waitresses used to go to the dining room. It being a college beer hall the area was frequented but guys taking a piss.

Susan came by while I was frying stuff and told me that my stash had somehow come loose and pills were all over the floor of the john and the hallway leading to the dinning room. I shit my pants!

People in suits would come into the shack for clams and to look at the Beatniks and pretty college girls. We naturally assumed that everyone in a suit was a narc. If a narc went to the john he would recognize what those pills were.

I went into the hall and picked up the several pills that were there and then into the bathroom and flushed them and the ones on the floor there too. The constant slamming of the bathroom door had dislodged the bag and pills had spilled out every time someone left the room. I was convinced I was toast and I spent the rest of my shift looking over my shoulder convinced one of the suits would come for me.

Jake, the bark tea drinker, became my bestest friend and was always after some pills. I never sold any of them, just gave them away to close friends. Jake was such a weirdo that I didn't want to have anything to do with him. But if he was determined to drink bark tea for a high he was equally determined to get some of those pills from me. I didn't like any of it one bit and finally when there was only a few pills left in the bag I gave him the whole bag. Jake was no longer my bestest friend and I was out of giving them away. I'm just not cut out for doing criminal things. I swear there's a neon sign on my forehead that flashes, "Liar" whenever I try to deceive someone, so I don't bother. It's just too damn hard to keep a lie going anyway.

I'm not sure what happened to Jake as he went in search for new highs. I would not be surprised about anything that happened to him. He was a loser from the get go. If it wasn't drugs then he would be a drunk. Some people are what they are and nothing will ever change them. I bet there are plenty of people who don't agree with me about that, but my opinion is based on my life experience; your results may vary.

You Better Start Praying, President Kennedy Has Been Shot...

Most people who were alive when Kennedy was assassinated remember where they were and what they were doing when they found out. It happened at 11:30 AM EST on November 22, 1963, I was 18 at the time and in class at Vocational High School on Syracuse's west side. My classroom at that moment was on the first floor almost directly across from the school office. One of the women who worked in the office opened our door, leaned in and said,

"You better start praying, President Kennedy has been shot."

We had no more information than that and it seemed like hours before we found out he was dead. At 18 my political views had not matured and I was neither a Democrat or Republican. Back then you had to be 21 to vote, so I wasn't even thinking about politics. But the Kennedy's were stars, not like presidents since then. Camelot was real to all of those in my age group. My parents were Republicans but they didn't preach to me that I remember.

After school we all raced home to the TV to find out more about the assassination. Back then news was by radio, newspapers or TV and TV was still fairly new by today's standards. The news trickled out to us and we were all in some other mental space for days afterwards. That night I went to Marshall Street to be with my friends. We sat on the grass at the cherry bomb intersection and just talked and talked about it. It was a warm night for November in

Syracuse and everyone was out and everyone was talking about it. We knew nothing of the who or why, all we knew was we had a new president in President Johnson and nobody liked him. He was old and not charismatic like Jack Kennedy.

The next days and weeks and then years were consumed by rumors and conspiracy theories about the assassination. Nobody really knew the truth or a truth anyone could really believe. The long drawn out Warren Commission Report that was supposed to clear it all up did not. After a while the Vietnam war took center stage again and Johnson bungled that. At my draft able age I didn't want to go. The war didn't seem to have a point and we weren't in it to win it. But that's another story for another time.

The only thing that comes close to the Kennedy assassination for me was on September 24, 1955. I was ten and President Eisenhower had a serious heart attack. I was home watching TV when the news came in. I remember the room, the TV in the corner, B&W of course, and sitting on the floor watching it when the news came on. It scared me but he lived through it and finished out his term.

I was in second grade when Ike ran for President in November 1952. Only 7 at the time, some of my friends and I saw a kiosk on our way to school. (They just called them booths back then, nobody knew what a kiosk was.) The lady in the booth was handing out, "I Like Ike" buttons and we each got one. We marched around the school's sidewalk in single file chanting, "I Like Ike, I Like Ike" and displaying our buttons. We didn't know why the hell we, "Liked Ike" but we had buttons that said we did and that's all that mattered. Ike was a Republican so my parents were pleased when I came home wearing my button. It became a part of my ensemble everyday when I went to school. Ike won and ran for two terms followed by Kennedy in 1960. Ike won WWII as a five star general in charge of the Allies and took office after war time President Harry Truman. His Vice President was Nixon who lost to Kennedy largely due to a horrible performance in the first televised TV debate. Nixon looked bad, no TV makeup and a five o'clock shadow. People who just heard the debate on the radio thought Nixon won. But Kennedy was the young good looking charismatic candidate and I guess you could say he won on looks alone.

Gas Balloons

This is one of those stories that has no beginning. By that I mean I don't know who started this crazy idea so I can't give credit or blame. Perhaps I started it and I don't want the blame for it. Thankfully, no one ever got hurt and that in itself is a miracle. Here is the outline. First get some empty dry cleaner bags, the long ones. A roll of toilet paper, an iron, some wooden match heads and some slow burning fuse. We made our own fuse with salt peter and string (I think) The top and bottom of the dry cleaner bag needs to be sealed. Do this by folding the toilet paper over the edge and using the iron to seal it. You will have to play with the irons settings to get this right. Be careful not to touch the plastic other than where the toilet paper is. Leave one corner unsealed, just big enough to fit over the gas pipe in your apartment or home. Now tape 5 or 6 match heads to the fuse (set for a 5 minute burn) and tape that to the side of the bag.

Now from here on it helps if you are really mind numbingly stupid. Take the open end of the bag and hold it around the gas pipe and turn on the gas until the bag is full. Tie a knot in the bag and take it outside. Light the fuse with a punk or a cigarette, not a match you idiot! And let go. Helps if there is no wind and no trees in sight and dark is a good idea too. In five minutes there will be a large yellow fireball that will light up the night sky. The entire bag will be instantly consumed except for the knot which during the day looks like a burning man parachuting out of a burning dirigible to on lookers. I speak from experience. Also that burning knot might land on your neighbors garage roof and give you fits for the 15 minutes it takes to burn out.

Now from this point on you have to be beyond stupid into the nether world of really quite dumb. Take three of these bags and two friends and stuff everything into the back of a TR-3 with the top up, yeah, I said up. Can't fit you say, sure it can … did it. Drive to the park and let them all go. Oh, and by the way, have that really stupid friend you brought along smoke a cigarette while on the drive to the park.

I'm well along writing the narrative of my life and I've written about some of the extra stupid things I did on the way to growing up. But I haven't written about them all yet. Putting this tome together forced me to rethink all of those things and the inescapable question I ask myself is how the hell I managed to stay alive through it all.

How To Get Away With Overusing My Fathers Car

Every Saturday night I borrowed my fathers car and every time he told me I could only go 100 miles and that I had to be back by 1AM. Every time I went more than 100 miles and I never got back by 1AM. Each Sunday he would bitch at me about my not following his rules and that he would not let me have the car next Saturday. But by the next Saturday he gave me the car again. This was our little drama that we played out each week until one week when something very unusual happened...

I got lucky and in the dark I left some evidence behind in my Dad's car. That Sunday he called me out to the garage looking very upset and confronted me with the evidence and asked if I had a girl in the car the night before. Faced with the overwhelming evidence I admitted I had. He broke into a big smile and jabbed me in the shoulder saying, "Way to go!" From that moment on whenever he asked me why I was late and put so many miles on the car I just inferred that I had a girl and he was happy. He must have thought I was some stud.

BANG! ZING! BANG!

My friend Leo's father always bought junk cars for fifty bucks and when they wore out he just bought another one. Usually you couldn't get a junked car registered but he had some connections that fixed it for him. When Leo would leave my house he would back out of my driveway into the street, put the car in neutral, floor the gas pedal and drop it into drive and burn rubber down the street.

One day I gave Leo a ride home in my fathers two week old Chrysler Newport. It was the kind with shift buttons on the dashboard. When I dropped Leo off I backed out of his driveway into the street, pushed the neutral button and gave it a little gas, I was too chicken to floor it. Then I punched the drive button… BANG! ZING! BANG! My heart stopped, but then the car started rolling so I thought all was OK. I came up to the stop sign and when the car downshifted… BANG! ZING! BANG! Shit! Then it started rolling again but every time I came to a stop… BANG! ZING! BANG! It did this whenever it downshifted into first when you came to a stop.

Our house on Herkimer Street had a garage behind the house that was down a long straight driveway. But you had to make a little jog to the left and then to the right to line up with the garage. My plan was to kill the engine before the car came to a stop and coast into the garage. BUT as I came by the end of the house I saw my father out of the corner of my eye over to the left hanging up clothes and it spooked me and I didn't get lined up with the garage.

I had to stop BANG! ZING! BANG!

My father turned around to look at me while holding a wet sheet up in front of him.

BANG! ZING! BANG! I backed up to get aligned with the garage.

BANG! ZING! BANG! I started forward, my father just stared, still holding that wet sheet up in front of him.

BANG! ZING! BANG! I came to a stop in the garage.

I got out of the car and came out of the garage. There was my father staring at me still holding that wet sheet. I'll never forget that look on his face as he waited patiently for my excuse … ah rather explanation for the BANG! ZING! BANG! I decided that the best course of action was to tell the truth … sort of. I told him about backing out of Leo's driveway, putting it in neutral, giving it some gas and dropping it in drive. However… I didn't tell him I did it on purpose. I told him I pushed the neutral button by mistake and when I gave it the gas and it didn't move realizing my mistake I pushed the drive button in a rush. Not a bad story for being under a lot of pressure eh? He bought it, or maybe he just said he did. If I had broken it then he would have had to pay to fix it.

It turned out that the transmission had a defect and was repaired under warranty. It was a good thing I discovered this for my Dad. Wouldn't it have been terrible if it happened to him on a desolate road in the middle of nowhere. Aren't I a good son and aren't you glad I'm not yours.

Spilling Beer on the Kid at the Flying Field

I got quite involved in flying radio controlled model airplanes. Every year the club I belonged to had a fly-in, where we invited other hobbyists from other clubs to come in and compete in various events. Their clubs would do the same. My summers were spent going to these fly-ins each weekend.

It required some preparation for the fly-in. We had to get the flying field spruced up, a concession stand set up and various other chores done the night before. On this particular Friday evening, when all the work was done, we were having a beer and started goofing off. We ran around shaking up the beer bottles and trying to squirt each other. One kid, about 16, who was not drinking because he was underage, got sprayed by me. I forget his name now but he was a nice kid. Nothing was mentioned at the time about any problems spraying beer on him would have.

The next day as we were getting everything set up for the days activities. I was at the main tent where all the activities were coordinated when I saw the boy from the night before and his elderly parents heading my way. Oblivious to any impending problems I greeted them like old friends but was met with a cold stare. I sensed something was wrong right away but I couldn't tell what it was. The mother, in an obviously agitated state, said that she was there to tell me off. That I knew that she had lost a son to a drunken driver and that I deliberately spilled beer on her remaining son to hurt her.

Obviously none of this was true but I knew instinctually that she was not in a state of mind to hear anything I had to say. I decided to say nothing for fear that it would further hurt her, but just to take whatever she needed to do to me. After a few moments they left leaving me quite shaken. One of my friends who had heard this exchange said that I did the right thing by not trying to defend myself and just let her vent. That didn't help because even though I did the 'right thing' I still hurt this family by my ignorance and that bothered me then and does to this day. Sometimes our innocent actions have consequences we can't imagine at the time we commit them. Another life lesson learned.

WAITING FOR THE STOP SIGN TO TURN GREEN

One night about 2 in the morning I was sitting at a stop sign bone tired. A cop car pulled up to my left and asked me.

"Did you know you just stopped at the red light back there, looked both ways and went on through it?"

To which I laughed and said. "That's nothing I'm waiting for this stop sign to turn green!"

He said. "We thought that's what you were doing." We all had a good laugh and I went on home.

THE CHURCH STEEPLE AND THE CABINET SHOP

I worked in a cabinet and Formica shop where we mostly made countertops, post formed countertops. The kind you see precut in home centers these days. One day a lightening bolt hit the church steeple across the road blowing bricks across the street and into the banks parking lot. Several days later a crew came to remove the steeple which I assume wasn't repairable. A disaster in the making. From our vantage point it was clear that the top of the crane was lower than the top of the steeple.

All day crews worked from the inside of the steeple cutting it loose with chain saws. Picture a folding umbrella as I describe the rest. They fashioned a cable around the bottom or wider part of the cone shaped steeple. It seemed obvious to me that as soon as they lifted on the cable the steeple would turn upside down. I assumed they knew what they were doing. As they were getting ready to do the deed I called the rest of the crew in the shop to the window to watch the show. It did worse than I thought. When the steeple broke free it did indeed turn upside down and then it collapsed like a folding umbrella, fell out of the loop of cable and came crashing down breaking a $20,000 stained glass window in the process. Sometimes the experts aren't that expert.

ISLAGIATT

is-la-gi-at

ISLAGIATT is on a sign in my garage that I point to when people wonder why I did some particularly odd thing. "It Seemed Like A Good Idea At The Time" and as I write about my life I realize that ISLAGIATT has been with me for a very long time. Does that mean that I'm impulsive, eager to take chances or just plain dumb? A bit of each probably. But I have no regrets, my life has been and continues to be an interesting experience, full of wonder, full of life. So, no regrets here but if I had it to do over…

THE TOILET PAPER MYSTERY

Sometimes random bits of information collide and only questions remain.

For example: I read a story about a fellow who was the maintenance man for a woman's college dorm. One comment stuck out. He said his biggest problem was keeping enough toilet paper in the bathrooms. Apparently the women used far more of it than men do. That's odd, I thought as I tried to image what other uses they could have for it beside the obvious one. Then at another point in time during a conversation that I wish I could remember the context of, a woman told me that she used just 6 sheets of paper each time. This does not compute, as the saying goes. So what happens to all the toilet paper in the women's dorm?

I guess I'll just chalk it up to one other thing we men are never supposed to understand about women. Hell, for all we know they're making paper machete dildos with the stuff.

You got a better idea?

Pop's Tale

Joe, Bill and Bob Hogg
The Infamous "Hogg Boys"

I can't attest to the veracity of this because I wasn't there and I wouldn't be surprised if Pop didn't embellish this a bit. But as I remember it, this is his tale.

He and his brothers were the terror of the town, always doing things that got them into trouble. They were known and not affectionally either, as the, "Hogg Boys."

They wanted to play a joke on the town constable, who apparently did them some wrong. (Probably caught them doing something bad) They hatched this complex scheme.

Pop was born in 1903 and I think he would have been a teenager so let's say it was 1920 or so. This is what he told me they did;

On a moonless night they took an oil drum, some carbide, a ford coil, spark plug, battery and a little bit of water and put that on the pitchers mound at the ball field next to the school. Then they strung a long piece of music wire from the equipment shed at the ball field to the bell tower on top of the school. In the bell tower they unhooked the clapper from the rope that went down to the main floor and barricaded the trap door to the bell tower and connected the music wire to the clapper. They climbed down the roof and onto the ground and assembled at the equipment shed.

The carbide was poured into the drum which had the spark plug installed and connected to a wire that went to the shed some hundred feet away. By the way carbide is what coal miners used in their lights in the mine. It looks like grey pebbles and when you add water to it you get acetylene gas, the stuff that's used for welding and it is very explosive. With everything set they all retreated to the shed. At about 2AM they connected the spark plug wire to the Ford coil and battery and the oil drum exploded blowing a sizable hole in the pitchers mound and waking everybody up.

Then in the dark of the shed they started clanging the bell. Being dark you couldn't see the wire running to the shed so they just stayed there and rang the bell. Everyone came out including the law but all their attempts to get into the bell tower failed. The constable, still in his long-johns, assumed someone had barricaded themselves in the tower.

He shouted, "Come down out of there of I'll shoot." All his attempts to get that non existent person to give up failed and he started shooting at the tower. All this did was make more noise both from the gun and the bullets hitting the bell. When it started to get light and the possibility someone would see the wire The Hogg Boys abandoned the shed and got away. They never found out who did it but everybody assumed it was the, "Hogg Boys."

I didn't hear this story until I was an adult. If I had known what kind of kid my Pop was I could have used that to get away with a lot more than I did. At the same time I assume I inherited this trait from my father. All of us boys tried mischievous tricks but nothing could top this.

POP THE CHARACTER

Known as 'Pop' or 'Dad' to us five boys. 'Uncle Bill' to my cousins, Pop was indeed a character. He was an old school salesman, told jokes and pressed the flesh. Not at all like the salesmen who would call at my dental lab. The character Willy Lomax in Death of a Salesman so reminds me of my Dad that I have never watched more than a few minutes of it. Just made me too sad. One time one of the companies he sold for got a young new sales manager who demanded detailed reports of what Pop was doing. Pop didn't like that, after all he was his own man, working for commissions and he didn't think the reports were worth the time he had to spend on them. But he did it, just once. After he got the details together he transcribed it to paper. It took many tries using different kinds of pens before he found the combination that would work on toilet paper. A few days after he sent it in the president of the company he'd been working for 17 years called him.

President: "Bill, I take it from your choice of paper you don't like doing the reports" They had a good laugh about it along with the president asking him how many tries if took and how long it took to write all that on toilet paper. I wouldn't be surprised to see that report in a frame somewhere.

They were old friends and the sales manager was a new, wet behind the ears, college kid who thought he knew everything. He might have, he just didn't understand what he knew.

Pop always had a variety of business cards to match any situation. A couple I really liked were:

The super small card which was about one quarter the size of a regular business card. It had the usual information on it with a tag line on the bottom that said words to the effect: "Sorry about the small card but I haven't had any orders from you in so long I can't afford a full size one."

The everything card. On it he listed every position from CEO on down under his name, the last one being, "Janitor" which every business owner could identify with.

He would stop down at the lab on his way out for a business trip and pull one card from this pocket and one from that. One of my employees said, "How many pockets you got in that damn coat?" But he had such a pleasant demeanor that it was impossible not to like him and he had a very loyal customer base and loyal employers too. All the ones he represented when he died made sure Mom got the commissions due him and likely a bit more too.

We had a good back and forth going all the time too. One year a particularly bad Christmas Day storm dumped three feet of snow on Syracuse. I was without a decent snow blower. The next day I called my friend Ron at the nearby garden store and asked him what kind of snow blower he had.

"I have one Ariens 8HP blower left and it's $699" He said.

Usually I could get a break from Ron but as it was early in the day and he had just the one left I knew any kind of a deal wasn't going to happen. Once he sold that one he was going home.

So I said, "If you can deliver it to the bottom of my driveway full of gas I'll take it"

The next day I was talking to Pop who was in the same dilemma as me and had to buy a snow blower. By chance he got the same 8HP one I had but from a different dealer.

"How big are the tires on yours?" he asked.

"8 inches." I said.

"Mmm, mine are 12 inches." He said.

"That's nice. Did you get the cigarette lighter on yours" I said.

"No I didn't" he said

"Does yours have the regular dashboard or the padded one like mine." He said

"The padded one ... with leather." I said

It went on like that until we were both laughing so hard we couldn't keep it up anymore.

One day Pop asked me to drive him to the airport. I just bought a new 1979 Cadillac Coupe Deville. One of the features it had was an automatic closing trunk. It would grab the trunk lid when you got it close and pull it tight. The selling point was that you could close it with just your elbow if your arms were full of groceries and you were heading into the house. I ran into an acquaintance who had one like mine and we compared notes. He cautioned me to be careful with that trunk thing. He said you could break it by slamming it like you would an ordinary trunk. And to be careful closing it with large objects in it.

He had loaded his snow blower in the trunk to bring it to the shop and... Well, you'll have to picture this. After he got it in he was leaning over to watch to see if there was enough clearance which it turned out there wasn't. The closer grabbed the lid and tried to pull the trunk closed which ended up putting a dent in the trunk lid. It was fixed when I saw it but it must have been embarrassing trying to explain a dent from the inside out.

I told you that so I could tell you this. (Ron Thomason of the Dry Branch Fire Squad said that)

My father called me to pick him up to take him to the airport. He hadn't seen my new Caddy and made some approving comments. He was a Chrysler man and drove the Chrysler Imperial. He loaded his stuff in my trunk and was about to slam it shut when I yelled, "No" He turned to look at me with a question on his face. I walked around him and slowly closed the trunk until it caught and closed the rest of the way by itself. "Oh" he said.

We got in the car with me driving. He sat down in the passenger seat, pointed at the passenger side door which was open and said, "Door ... close" Nothing happened and he turned to me and said, "Oh, yours doesn't do that?"

On the way to the airport he asked me to stop at the post office where he had a PO box for his business. As I drove in the lot he said, "Pull into the handicapped parking spot, it's closer" "I don't want to do that" I said and he said, "That's okay, I'll limp" I pulled in and he got out of the car and walking into the post office with a highly exaggerated limp, got his mail.

He was a fun guy to hang out with and I obviously miss him a lot.

If you decide to write a retrospective like this be prepared to go through a range of emotions, from sad to very happy. At least that's how it's been for me. I loved my Dad but he was irritating too. I guess that's just part of this existence we have. I wonder how many of us, if given the chance, would pick different parents. I know I wouldn't, how about you?

Here we have Pop at the camp, test burning a barrel stove he made.

Pop made this stove on an old lawnmower base so he could roll it in and out of the cabin. Sounds good on paper but the heat from the stove melted the tires. Right after he made it he was rolling it into the cabin to test burn it. I looked at the paint on the barrel and suggested he do that outside. Here he is doing just that. But crude as it was it worked for years and threw off lots of heat. Years later I made one to heat my pole barn at the lake and it worked well too. As hard as I tried I couldn't argue with success.

Memorable Characters that Changed my Life

Most of the characters that changed my life did so not by what they did but rather by what they were. In a way you could say they led by example. We meet many people as we go through life. Most of them are nothing more than scenery that has little effect on us. However, some people stand out and influence us in ways that we only see looking back. Our parents are by far the most memorable, followed by teachers and friends. Beyond those influences are those special people that we tell stories about or quote or brag that we know.

I've listed many of them on these pages and I probably missed a few too.

Broken Leg, Back, Ribs, Ruptured Spleen and Exploded Intestines

When I was 19 I got my father to co-sign a loan so I could buy a car. But somehow I ended up with a 200CC Bultaco motorcycle. Within minutes of getting it, I was driving down Eire Boulevard and passed my father. He had this odd look of surprise on his face. I just smiled back and drove on and started working on my story.

I loved riding that bike, the speed, the acceleration. One day I came down Crouse Ave on the hill at 90 MPH. It dawned on me that if someone walked out on the street or a car backed out of a driveway there would be no stopping. I hit the brakes but it took two full blocks to slow it down. I decided to confine my reckless driving to more open spaces.

It was May and cold and I would stop in at the Savoy restaurant to warm up. I had been having trouble with the headlights, every now and then they would just turn off. I would diddle with the switch and they would come back on.

A girl in the Savoy asked me to take her for a ride and I said fine. We went for a long ride out to Jamesville and beyond. I was coming down the long winding hill that leads into Jamesville when the lights went out. It was pitch black and I couldn't see a damn thing. My hands were cold as I fumbled with the light switch while visions of ending up in the deep ditch on the side of the road went through my head. I couldn't get the switch to work with my cold hand so I looked up and could just make out the slight difference between the trees and sky and steered by that. After a few moments I finally got the lights to work and I was exactly in the center of my lane.

Days later I was out riding with a friend who also had a bike. We decided to do some cross country riding and started following paths through the woods. It was dark and we didn't know or care where we were going because we were having fun. After a bit we came out on an abandoned railroad line. The tracks and ties were gone but the gravel ballast was still there. It was smooth so we started high tailing it down the roadbed. My bike was faster than his so when I got quite a bit ahead of him so I stopped and waited for him. He caught up to me and we sat there talking.

After a while we noticed a car coming towards us from the side. Must be a road there we thought. The car was coming down a small hill and was below us. He passed by us within 20 feet, but he went under the underpass that was still there for the railroad. The car lights showed us for the first time the granite walls of the underpass just a few feet in front of us. But when they took out the rail and ties they also took out the bridge. There was nothing left but a 20 foot drop-off down to the road. We didn't see it because of the dark. If I had not stopped where I did I would surely have gone off the abutment and splattered into the opposite wall. It is also likely my friend would have done the same. We didn't say a word but boy that sure puckered our assholes. We rode our bikes down the embankment onto the road and went home.

Wreck!

When I look back on my life I think of those things that caused me to go off in a different direction, that changed my life forever. Sometimes those things are small and over a long time. Others are more abrupt much like a ball hitting a post. My first life changing event happened when I was 12 and I broke my leg crashing into a taxi cab. My sporting days were over and I went in a different direction. The same thing happened when I was 19 and I wrecked my Bultaco motorcycle.

I went out for a lunchtime ride from where I was working at the TV repair place. I drove out W. Genesee St. and turned left on Thomson Road and out past Carrier Corp, around Carrier Circle and headed back to work. The bike was still new and I loved riding it and did so whenever

I could. I don't remember what happened, but I was told after the fact.

I was driving east on W. Genesee Street, probably going too fast. As I approached the small shopping center where I worked the car in front of me slowed and started to turn right into the parking lot. I pulled to the left to go around him. At the same time a guy driving west who didn't see me behind the turning car turned left to follow him in. As I pulled around the car in front of me I crashed into him. My left leg broke where it contacted his bumper and I received internal injuries from the impact. My body bounced off the front of his car and landed next to a car waiting to exit the parking lot unto W. Genesee Street. I was unconscious. I was not wearing my helmut because it didn't fit well.

My first memory after the accident was being on a gurney on my back looking at the ceiling lights as I was wheeled down a hallway. Then nothing until I was in a room with concerned people looking down on me. Then very little until I was in my hospital bed. For the next day or two many people came to visit, friends, family, etc. That's still a blur.

I don't remember the pain but I remember I was in a lot of pain. After a day or so I could feel something wasn't right in my gut, it just felt wrong. My doctor came in to talk to me. He said they thought I had a ruptured spleen and that they wanted to operate on me. I asked what my chances were of surviving the operation and he said, "Fifty/fifty." I asked him what would happen if they didn't operate and he said, "You'll die." Faced with those choices I agreed to the operation. I didn't know it at the time but my parents had already given them the go ahead to operate.

Along with those injuries I also broke some small bones on my back and some ribs. My left side from my hip down was eggplant purple. I was in bad shape.

This was the second major life changing event of my life. What happened after the operation, my recovery and major changes of my life are the subject for Part Two of this series of books.

Postmortem

Well, that's it. We've come to the end of Part One. As I look back on my life to this point I wonder how it compares to yours. Many people have far more interesting lives than mine and I think that I've had a more interesting life than others. But it's not a competition, it's life. You get out of it what you put in. I look at everything through the lens of a story. No matter what happens to me, it is okay as long as I can make a story out of it to tell my friends.

Even back in the days of building model airplanes when I would crash and destroy a plane that I spent weeks and sometimes months building. I never thought of it as a loss. I learned something while I was building it, some new technique or experimented with some new material. When it crashed I would examine the wreckage very carefully to see if things like the shock absorbing material I put around the radio worked and how well it did it's job. I also learned how various glues and structural elements survived the crash. In every event save for death, something can be learned. When I had my dental lab, I would go for weekend seminars and I considered the time well spent if I learned just one thing because I could use that one thing forever.

As I've grown older my temper has softened, my patience increased along with my love for life. There was a time a few years back when it dawned on me that I was just looking for the easiest way to die. I turned that around and made some drastic changes in my life and now I'm in a great place.

I enjoyed writing this book more than I thought I would. I expected it to be drudgery and it turned out to be a joy to do. As I wrote about things that happened decades ago my memory improved and things came back like they happened yesterday. I was able to enjoy those events all over again. Even the bad things, the broken legs, and worse came back for the fun things that came from them. It also made me consider how and in what way my life would have changed if those seemingly little things I did were done differently. You can't change your past, you can only use your experience to change your future.

Life is an endless learning process ... and life, if you do it right, can be a funny thing.

The End

Check your bookstore for the next in this series of books, "Yikes, you can see my underpants!, Part Two"

For updates check the website, blog at:

http://www.FrankHogg.com

I use the blog to post updated information on works in progress and other news and resources. In addition you'll find an "Extras" page to supplement each book with information and pictures not found in the book.

Email me: Frank@FrankHogg.com with any questions or suggestions.

Thank you very much for allowing me to share my life's stories with you.

Sincerely,

Frank Hogg

www.ingramcontent.com/pod-product-compliance
Lightning Source LLC
LaVergne TN
LVHW051508080426
835509LV00017B/1977